The
Exercise Habit

The Exercise Habit

James Gavin, PhD
Sport Psychologist

Leisure Press
Champaign, Illinois

Library of Congress Catalogin-in-Publication Data

Gavin, James, 1942-
 The exercise habit / James Gavin.
  p. cm.
 Includes bibliographical references (p.) and index.
 ISBN 0-88011-457-6
 1. Exercise--Psychological aspects. I. Title.
 GV481.2.G38 1992
 613.7'1--dc20   91-21042
                                                     CIP
 ISBN: 0-88011-457-6

Acquisitions Editor: Brian Holding; **Developmental Editor:** Lori Garrett; **Assistant Editors:** Dawn Levy, Moyra Knight, Elizabeth Bridgett; **Copyeditor:** Wendy Nelson; **Proofreaders:** Kathy Bennett, Dawn Levy; **Indexer:** Barbara Cohen; **Production Director:** Ernie Noa; **Typesetters:** Yvonne Winsor, Kathy Boudreau-Fuoss; **Text Design:** Keith Blomberg; **Text Layout:** Yvonne Winsor, Tara Welsch; **Cover Design:** Tim Offenstein; **Illustrations:** Timothy Stiles, Gretchen Walters; **Printer:** Versa Press

Leisure Press books are available at special discounts for bulk purchase for sales promotions, premiums, fund-raising, or educational use. Special editions or book excerpts can also be created to specification. For details, contact the Special Sales Manager at Leisure Press.

Printed in the United States of America   10 9 8 7 6 5 4 3

Leisure Press
A Division of Human Kinetics
P.O. Box 5076, Champaign, IL 61825-5076
1-800-747-4457

Canada: Human Kinetics, Box 24040, Windsor, ON N8Y 4Y9
1-800-465-7301 (in Canada only)

Europe: Human Kinetics, P.O. Box IW14, Leeds LS16 6TR, England
0532-781708

Australia: Human Kinetics, Unit 5, 32 Raglan Avenue, Edwardstown 5039, South Australia
(08) 371 3755

New Zealand: Human Kinetics, P.O. Box 105-231, Auckland 1
(09) 309-2259

To Peter A. Simeone, S.J.
(1932-1989)
—Priest, doctor, poet, and friend

"It is only with the heart that one can see rightly:
what is essential is invisible to the eye."
(Antoine de Saint-Exupery, *The Little Prince*)

CONTENTS

PREFACE

What does exercise look like? In the fitness world, it can look like sculpted bodies on chrome-plated machines or Day-Glo running suits breezing through the park. Maybe it takes shape in half-awake beings trying to imitate the moves of flashy TV aerobics instructors. For traditionalists it could look like walking the dog, raking the lawn, or chores around the house.

Whatever exercise looks like, you probably have a sense you are doing too little of it. Recent estimates by the U.S. Public Health Service suggest that 90% of adult Americans don't get sufficient exercise. You have your reasons: It's impossible to make time; it costs too much; you're too tired or embarrassed.

New Year's resolutions to exercise wear off by Valentine's Day. Your doctor's warning weakens when you see the paunch hanging over his belt. Your friends don't help when they slip that extra serving onto your plate. The whole world seems to conspire against you.

Willpower alone won't do it—and it's demoralizing to discover that you can't follow through on your intentions. So you end up telling yourself it's too late to start. The lie becomes apparent when you see someone twice your age out there doing it. You double your rationalizations.

But then you decide to give it another chance. You pick up this book in the hope you will discover something new, something that will make it easier or at the very least will make your decision stick. You are searching for that bond-forever exercise glue.

Well, keep reading. One thing is guaranteed: When you read this book, your perception of exercise will change forever. You will come to see it as one of the most powerful tools for self-transformation available today. You will realize exercise isn't something you do for your body alone—it influences your thoughts, your feelings, your entire being. It re-creates you inside and out.

The Exercise Habit is your personal road map to developing a lifelong exercise commitment. You will appreciate how you can satisfy your life interests and motives through exercise. Like a perfume that mixes with your body scents to create a unique fragrance, your journey of self-discovery through this book will enable you to design an exercise program that fits your personal profile.

Think of this book as a complete workout—with a warm-up, high-impact exercises, and a cool-down. *The Exercise Habit* is divided into three parts. **Part I** gets you warmed up to the idea of bringing exercise fully into your life. You haven't been able to stick with your past decisions, because you didn't realize how exercise can satisfy so many of your lifelong motivations. **Part I** helps you understand what you will gain, as well as the reasons why you have avoided exercise in the past.

Part II takes you through a high-impact, step-by-step analysis of 18 specific motivations drawn from three general categories—body motives, psychological motives, and social motives—that help you develop a commitment to the exercise habit. You learn how exercise can help with, for example, the desire to manage your weight, the psychological need for self-esteem, and the desire to gain control over roller-coastering social relationships. Depending on your test scores, you are directed toward different fitness plans that hold the most promise for meeting your needs. The exercise program you are guided to develop will be uniquely yours, catering to all the aspects of your personality that you want to nurture.

Part III is the cool-down. You get the tools to make things gel. By coming to understand the ups and downs of developing an exercise habit, you learn what you need on this journey, and your path is clearer. Prepare for the course by getting solid information about potential obstacles and pitfalls you may face as you integrate fitness into your life. You discover how to plan and what to expect. You will realize that self-acceptance is the key to getting through the hard times.

Knowing all the ways your life preferences can be gratified by the *right* fitness program will make it easier for you to begin and stay with it. *The Exercise Habit* gives you all the tools to analyze your motivations, plan your program, and chart your course toward a fitness lifestyle. The promise of this book is to make you deeply aware of your motivations to exercise and to teach you how to connect with the right personal program so that you can stay with it for life.

Connect with your inner drives. Challenge yourself to change in ways you have always wanted to change. Deepen your desire for play and excitement. Discover dimensions of exercise that make it your perfect expression of mind, body, and spirit. In time, exercise will unveil its most precious gift—the feeling of being lustfully alive.

ACKNOWLEDGMENTS

Writing a book of this nature requires different kinds of input. There was the ocean's riptide in the summer of 1949 that provoked my first swimming lesson. A gift of muscle-building pulleys on Christmas of 1951 initiated my interest in body building. Then, there was the time my swimming coach instructed me to hold my ankles to avoid taking a false start. I ended up in the hospital with a badly banged head—that prompted my running career. All this is background—important as it was, it served mainly to point me in the direction of this book. The immediate task of writing it was fostered by friends and family. Hanging around with aspiring jocks, real jocks, and antijocks filled me with anecdotes for my writing. I hope my friends forgive me for taking liberty with their passions.

My sister has threatened to write *The Exercise Habit II: Undoing It* to get even with me for the "vicious lies" about her and my brother in the prologue. To her credit, she nonetheless suffered through editing various drafts of this book (I think she got even).

My children kept me on track. Whenever I pondered the hardships of a "fitness lifestyle," I would watch Jacob skateboarding or Susannah turning blue with delight in the lake. Even my "reluctant athlete," Jessica, would return from her daily runs with joyous gasps. They knew instinctively that movement was pleasure. I thank them for reminding me.

Just when I thought I had it right, I learned all about the myopia of writers working feverishly against deadlines. My editor, Lori Garrett, gently coaxed me into a new perspective on the book and a reconstruction of certain sections. Her feedback and support were critical and greatly appreciated.

Most of all, I want to acknowledge my friend and inspirational guide, Nettie Jane Glickman. It wasn't just the thousands of tasks she did to help me throughout this ecstatic ordeal of writing, but the multiple roles she played of Buddha, buddy, scout, editor, and itinerant reporter. Her gift of gab opened the doors to many people's stories, and her sense of humor brought out the divine comedy in it all.

PROLOGUE

The Ups and Downs of a Fitness Fanatic

I had no intention of becoming a committed recreational athlete, but as I look back over my life I can see that the seeds were planted early. My childhood play developed into lifelong passions, and the values I derived from physical activity blossomed over the years.

I grew up in a family where no one exercised. We lived in the heart of New York City—Manhattan. My parents were immigrants. Their parents were farmers. Maybe they thought exercise was frivolous—or at best something that should be connected to earning a living. Or perhaps they were simply too tired to think about exercise at the end of their long days. My brother and sister didn't exercise either. They were bookworms. They studied for hours with heads propped up under gooseneck lamps. Everyone in a family has to find a special niche, and so maybe it was preordained that I would end up a fitness fanatic.

I was a street kid. I loved the great outdoors. I got high on carbon monoxide. I relished the excitement. There was nothing like being chased down the wrong street in the wrong neighborhood to get my adrenaline going. How many of our great sprinters made their debut in some darkened alley with the neighborhood athletic committee on their tails? How many quarterbacks first learned their zigzag patterns dodging cars on Broadway? Life was great, and it didn't matter that there were no awards for surviving a trip to the grocery store or for winning a game of stickball in the middle of Columbus Avenue. It was just fun to be out there, in motion, part of the noise, the laughter, the primal pulse of the city.

In those days, we didn't have skateboards. We had scooters made from milk crates, a 2-by-4 liberated from a derelict building, and an old roller skate. There weren't too many baseball diamonds, either. We played ball on the streets—in between green lights.

I almost forgot—there was also work. It was a time when you could get a job just by asking. I delivered laundry on a bike with an enormous front basket. Every day after school, I rode the city streets with bundles of laundry piled so high I had to stand on the pedals to see over them.

Somewhere along the line I became a swimmer. There's a theory in psychology about how people choose things they fear most—like the stuttering Demosthenes becoming a great orator, or Hal Connolly, handicapped from birth with a bad left arm, who became an Olympic gold medalist in the hammer throw. It's a way of slaying your personal dragons. My dragon was a riptide at Rockaway Beach that wanted to convert me into fish food. Big surprise—when I hit high school athletics, I went out for the swim team.

I wasn't a great swimmer. In fact, I was pretty mediocre by national standards. I worked hard, and certainly had all the hopes, fears, and pains of more successful swimmers—but I never made the Olympics. So, after finishing my last race in college, I hung up my tank suit forever—or so I thought.

My first year in graduate school was an adjustment, but I made the shift from jock to recreational athlete without too much trauma. I was fortunate. I had a roommate who loved to run mountains, and I couldn't allow him to have all that fun by himself. Besides, he had one fatal flaw. He was an even runner, and in the last quarter mile, I was always able to smoke him. When you've been a competitive athlete, it's hard to let opportunities like that go by.

I changed schools my second year of graduate study. Back to the city. No more roommate. The lovehandles grew. When I finished graduate school 4 years later, I wasn't exactly a couch potato, but I had the shape of one. Even so, I prided myself on being among the first to jog regularly in Central Park—and survive.

My first job after graduate school seemed to leave no time for workouts. *Workouts?* I don't think the word was even in the vocabulary at that point. I traveled a lot, and I know I never considered taking my running shoes on business trips. Bathing suit, maybe, but compared to what I carry these days, the thought of packing exercise gear for my daily dose never crossed my mind.

It was only after I began my second job that I took full stock of my corpus grandiosum. I was 6-foot-1 and pushing the 200-pound mark. Some said I was impressive, but I felt fat and out of shape. I was living on a farm in Colorado, and I began running "around the block" each day. The block was 4 miles long around the perimeter, and sometimes I would double the dose. The longer runs felt so much better, mostly when I finished.

A constant diet of running hurt. My body ached, especially my joints. It seemed like an awful lot to go through simply for a sleek physique. Yet I knew I didn't want to make swimming a habit again. I had had enough of chlorinated eyes and blanched, burning skin. The answer to the question of what to do that was fun and healthy eluded me. Remember, this was at a time when people didn't obsess about exercise, when "fun runs" hadn't entered the lexicon of oxymorons, when Jane Fonda was renowned for antiwar marches and not aerobics, and when shoe stores carried only one or two brands of running shoes, both in the range of $19.95. It was the early 1970s. We were a nation preoccupied with things other than percent body fat and $\dot{V}O_2$max. There were things like Vietnam and Watergate and the Women's Movement. There were no fitness gurus. Even though Charles Atlas still leeched off the fantasies of scrawny, bashful boys, there were no sports medicine clinics or other places you could go for solid advice about what to do with your fashionably unfit body.

What I needed was a reasonable alternative to compressing my spinal disks and wearing out the cartilage in my knees through a daily routine of running. It must have been fate that in trying to find a t'ai chi class, which in those days was a rarity, I wandered into a modern dance studio. It intrigued me. A funny thing happened, however, when I took my first class. My body wouldn't cooperate. For all my self-proclaimed coordination, I couldn't do pirouettes. I also couldn't stretch or reach or bend the way my classmates could. I felt totally frustrated, but hooked nonetheless. Sure, I knew "real men" didn't wear leotards, but there was something here that was more challenging than anything I had tried before. I was psyched.

I started with two classes a week and gradually built to a daily routine. Living in Colorado I didn't have much competition when the local dance troupes held auditions (cowboys definitely don't wear leotards!). So I performed from time to time, getting high on stage fright and feeling great about my newfound talent. I occasionally ran, cycled, swam, and, of course, played softball when the season came around, but dance was my thing.

It changed suddenly. I tore a leg muscle in a class. Insufficient warm-up, or maybe I was too enthusiastic. Whatever the cause, I was in a state of shock. It took 6 months to heal, and then my other leg went out in sympathy. From that time on, it was like flipping a coin to determine which leg would give way in a class. I couldn't leap. I couldn't jump. I was finished. Well, who did I think I was anyway? I had a full-time job, a family, and lots of other obligations that gobbled up my days. I didn't have time for a semipro career as a dancer. But what was next? I wanted to keep active.

The '80s! Aerobics! The dance exercise decade! Running had peaked, triathlons were considered fanatical, high-tech weight systems promised more than they delivered, but aerobics held center stage in the fitness world. I thought, why not? It was a little like dance and a lot more of a workout in a shorter period of time. I put myself on a regular diet of aerobics. Being careful about footwear and dance floors kept me injury free. Then I tried teaching aerobics for added excitement. And so it went over the years—from high- to low-impact and then high/low combo, on to body shaping and stretch and flex, and eventually coming full circle with circuit training, a modern-day resurrection of the old P.E. class. I did it all.

And now? Interestingly, I am back to basics, back to my roots. Back to swimming in freshwater lakes, running through the countryside and pushing my bike up and down hills. Some call it cross-training. I just call it another way of staying fit and having fun.

Why? Really, Why?

Read between the lines. That's what I try to do—to find out what it's all about. Your story will be different from mine. In one sense, I feel lucky—lucky to have "the habit." There are times when I thought I had it too much, and other times when I didn't have it enough, and then there were periods when I just worked out and didn't even think about it. The bottom line is that I *like* exercise. I feel good when I'm doing it, and I enjoy its many benefits. I can cross-country ski all day and still go to work the next morning. I can compete in triathlons. I can take an aerobics class and not trip over my feet when hit with a new piece of choreography. I can even have swimming races with my kids without asking for a head start.

But what is it really all about? It was little more than a century ago that the Industrial Revolution catapulted us from our benignly predictable path to a high-speed turnpike with unforeseen crossings. The human body became more or less superfluous. Work that had been synonymous with physical effort was transformed to mental effort or, at its worst, to a kind of mind-numbing twilight zone. Because our bodies waited while our minds worked, we had to include something called *exercise* in our leisure time, but most people never seemed to get around to it.

In its *Healthy People 2000* report, the U.S. Public Health Service estimates that less than 10% of the U.S. adult population currently exercises regularly. What's regular exercise? According to the American College of Sports Medicine, it amounts to about 30 minutes every other day. If we average it out, Americans might exercise about 5 minutes a day, taking into account house chores, the annual fishing trip, and the Fourth of July softball game.

Reports on the fitness levels of American youth are also discouraging. The next generation shows considerable declines in fitness tests compared to their parents' generation. And it isn't helped by the fact that only one state, Illinois, requires physical education for kindergartners through 12th-graders.

How is it that in a time when there is so much talk about fitness, diet, and health, we have such extremes—those who are fanatical, like the ultramarathoners and aerobics zombies, versus those who sweat only when the air conditioning breaks down? Is it genetics that makes some of us like to pump iron and smash little black balls, or do we get conditioned into becoming lifelong jocks?

Learning to Love It

A woman I know had never exercised in her life—until she turned 45. Jody was completely against it, thinking it a bore and waste of time. Now she says with a smile, "I'm an athlete." How did this transformation take place? She told me it came with a number of changes roughly translated as the "midlife crisis"—kids grown, husband engrossed in his career, her searching for a new identity. She was an attractive woman, but felt sluggish and out of shape. Her husband was an avid polo player, tennis star, and golf junkie. She felt more and more left out.

Jody tried exercising at home. That didn't work—too monotonous. She joined a health club—that didn't work either. She lasted through three aerobics classes and gave up—too robotic for her tastes. Fortunately, there was a trainer in her club who worked with people on an individual basis. She hired him in a last-ditch effort. Having someone to run with, to motivate her during those moments of weakness, and to guide her through the mysteries of weight training was what she needed.

She's a regular now. In fact, Jody complains about not having enough time to exercise. Unfortunately, she says, she has to earn a living, and so no Ironman Triathlon this year.

What motivated her is not entirely obvious. She was disturbed by a steady progression of dress sizes. Her cellulitis seemed terminal. She envied the fun her husband had in his sports. Her life had lost some of its purpose—the "empty nest" syndrome. She yearned for physical excitement. In sum, her motivations were a complex mixture that fueled a rather dramatic change in lifestyle and health attitudes.

She jokes now about running with her husband, who pants and wheezes on the uphill while she carries on a steady chatter. These days, her kids go to *her* sporting events, the latest of which was a bike-run biathlon. Jody feels great about herself, better than she has in years. And she looks terrific. The payoffs are obvious.

Jody's story is in large part the message of this book. It tells us we don't have to be born into it, we don't need a long history of sports involvement, and we don't even have to like it when we start. We do have to find a way of beginning and of nurturing the *exercise habit*—the rest will take care of itself.

P·A·R·T · I

MOTIVATION AND THE EXERCISE HABIT

CHAPTER 1

EXERCISE:
WE WANT TO—
BUT WE DON'T

"Almost one in two Americans dies of cardiovascular disease."
AMERICAN HEART ASSOCIATION

"Fewer than 10% of Americans older than 18 years meet the criteria for exercise proposed in the 1990 objectives for the nation."
JOURNAL OF THE AMERICAN MEDICAL ASSOCIATION

"American youth are getting fatter, not fitter—the trend is ominous."
CHRYSLER FUND—AMATEUR ATHLETIC UNION TESTING PROGRAM

Boom or Bust?

From the pages of the *Wall Street Journal* to articles in *Time* and *Newsweek*, we read about the demise of the fitness boom. We are inundated with reports of the decline in running, the retreat from aerobics, and the fadism of fitness. Athletic injuries abound. From tennis elbow to knee injuries and tendinitis, our pursuit of fitness has left us lined up at the sports clinic doors. The National Institutes of Health estimate that every year 17 million health-conscious Americans sustain injuries while working out and trying to keep fit.

Experts like New York cardiologist Dr. Henry Solomon, author of *The Exercise Myth*, tell us we really don't have to exercise, anyway. It isn't necessary for health—and may, in fact, overstress the heart. Dr. Neil Coplan, a cardiologist at Lenox Hill Hospital in New York, agrees. He believes the most serious risk of excessive exercise is damage to the heart. So, it's back to the sanity of Saturday afternoon naps, a welcome respite from pounding out the miles in a local "fun run."

"DO YOU REALLY THINK THIS IS A GOOD IDEA?"

Should we believe exercise is a bust? Some people do, but the weight of evidence is largely against that claim. The fitness boom is alive and well, thriving in forms never imagined by our forerunners who jogged around the block under the cloak of dark. Reports by the National Sporting Goods Association indicate that participation declined by 5% to 20% in running, swimming, tennis, calisthenics, and racquetball between 1984 and 1987. However, other sports picked up the slack. Nearly 17 million more people were walking for exercise in 1987 than in 1984—an increase of 40%. Aerobics went into an injury-fueled tailspin in the mid-'80s, but was resurrected by the advent of low-impact classes that appealed to an even wider audience. A recent Canadian study found that the proportion of people who followed a physically active lifestyle increased from 56% to 75% between 1981 and 1988. Nowhere was fitness's popularity more manifest than in the explosion of female participation. In May 1990 more than 10,000 women ran in the L'Eggs Mini Marathon in Central Park, compared to 78 women who ran in 1978!

Exercise extremism was given new meaning in the eighties. As the decade ended, five states boasted 100-mile races. The cultish Hawaiian Ironman Triathlon was imitated in similar events across the United States and in four foreign countries. Even the standard for athletic endurance, the 26.2-mile marathon, became a mid-length race as over 300 running contests per year exceeded this traditional distance. One race, the Badwater 146, took competitors from the lowest, hottest point in the U.S., across Death Valley to the highest point in the lower 48, a total of 146 miles.

In *Bodies: Why We Look the Way We Do (And How We Feel About It)* sociologist Barry Glassner offered some sobering statistics about our fitness passions: In 1987 Americans spent $5 billion on membership fees to health clubs; sales of exercise equipment increased from $5 million in

1977 to $738 million in 1987; and athletic shoe sales totaled over $6 billion. The National Sporting Goods Association estimated that sales of all sporting goods and recreational transport equipment totaled $33.7 billion in 1987. According to observers like Glassner, this was just the tip of the iceberg.

We have become a nation obsessed with youth, health, and fitness. Fat people are outcast. Smokers are shunned. Muscle is *in*. We don't want to look our age—we certainly don't want to feel it. Whether it is a Nautilus ad proclaiming "Fitness is everything" or the local paper's health columnist proffering fitness facts, we are immersed in a sea of information about what we should do to look and feel healthy. Virtually every major magazine has a section on fitness. Even the hallmark of suburban America, *Better Homes and Gardens*, has a sporty column on exercise and health. It's the new consciousness. We have to be aware of what we are doing to our bodies from the moment we wake up until our bedtime rituals.

Most of Us Try—Once in a While

We get the message. "It's a good idea to exercise." So what do we do? We try. The sun is shining, the air is crisp, so we go out for a walk. We may get more ambitious and try something else. We like diversity. Americans have virtually limitless opportunities for exercising, and we take advantage of them—at least once in a while. The National Sporting Goods Association estimates sports' popularity based on whether people say they participated in the activity once or more during the year (see Table 1.1). This tells us not how fit we are, but rather what we are drawn toward and on which activities we are willing to spend money. It helps us understand the values we have about leisure-time recreation and what we find enjoyable.

The large numbers of people who engage in recreational sports each year obscures the more fundamental answer we are seeking: How committed are we to making fitness part of our lives? If we are willing to try all these activities and to spend money on expensive equipment and clothing, what stops us from developing the exercise habit? Why do we lose the spark?

Answering this question is what this book is all about. It is encouraging to realize that most of us want to get started. It makes the task a little easier. The upcoming chapters will show you how to keep going, what to expect when you take on an exercise commitment, and what activities are best suited to your personal needs.

Understanding the Payoffs

Before we take a close-up of your motivational connections to the exercise world, let's consider the benefits you can expect from participating in a

Table 1.1   1989 Sports Participation

How many Americans participated in the activity more than once
(In millions of people 7 years of age or older)

Rank	Activity	Number in millions
1	Swimming	70.5
2	Exercise walking	66.6
3	Bicycling	56.9
4	Fishing	46.5
5	Camping	46.5
6	Bowling	40.8
7	Exercise/equipment	31.5
8	Billiards/pool	29.6
9	Boating (motor)	29.0
10	Basketball	26.2
11	Aerobic exercising	25.1
12	Volleyball	25.1
13	Running/jogging	24.8
14	Hiking	23.5
15	Golf	23.2
16	Softball	22.1
17	Rollerskating	21.5
18	Tennis	18.8
19	Hunting with firearms	17.7
20	Dart throwing	17.4
21	Baseball	15.4
22	Calisthenics	15.1
23	Football	14.7
24	Table tennis	13.7
25	Backpacking	11.4
26	Soccer	11.2
27	Alpine skiing	11.0
28	Water skiing	10.8
29	Horseback riding	10.1
30	Canoeing	9.4
31	Racquetball	8.2
32	Skateboarding	7.5
33	Ice/figure skating	7.0
34	Archery	5.6
35	Cross-country skiing	4.9
36	Sailing	4.7
37	Scuba	2.0
38	Snowboarding	1.6
39	Ice hockey	1.5
40	Rugby	0.3

From National Sporting Goods Association, Mt. Prospect, Illinois, 1989.

regular fitness program. Countless scientific studies say you'll be a winner if you take on a sensible exercise commitment.

The Physical Side

Maybe you don't need to be convinced, but in case you do, there are strong arguments from the medical profession concerning the health benefits of regular fitness participation. A consensus of leading medical scientists at the First International Conference on Exercise, Fitness, and Health held in 1988 concluded that regular physical exercise promotes health as well as preventing certain diseases.

Evidence of health benefits from exercise is vast. The following summary of research indicates some of the ways exercise might serve to improve your life.

Weight Management.   The most widely recognized effect of regular exercise is weight management. Exercise is considered a critical ingredient in most weight-loss programs. Dieting alone has been shown to be far less effective than dieting plus exercise. On the other hand, there is good evidence showing that exercise alone can produce and maintain substantial weight loss. The American College of Sports Medicine generally recommends that the best path to weight loss is a medically supervised program of dieting coupled with exercise.

People who diet often suffer the notorious yo-yo effect of a loss-gain cycle. This may be due to the depression of metabolic rate produced by severe caloric restriction. According to scientists at the University of California's Food Intake Laboratory, daily exercise can reverse the drop in metabolic rate produced by dieting.

The consensus seems to be that if your goal is weight reduction, adding exercise to a weight management plan will enable you to lose pounds, keep them off, and resume a less restrictive dietary pattern through the continuation of your exercise plan.

Aging.   In 1986 Dr. Ralph Paffenbarger, an epidemiologist at Stanford University, uncovered evidence that regular exercisers live longer than their sedentary peers. In addition to this benefit, research summarized at the 1988 international conference showed that regular exercise keeps us feeling and behaving younger than our years. The physiological explanation for this effect is that normally our ability to take in oxygen drops by about 10% a decade from ages 20 to 60. Exercise training slows this decline, especially during the 5th and 6th decades, allowing us to maintain the vigor and strength of someone 10 to 15 years younger.

Atherosclerosis.   Narrowing of the arteries is a disease that afflicts millions of Americans. It comes about through the buildup of fatty substances, cholesterol, and cellular wastes. Medical scientists have now identified how exercise can help us reduce the chances of suffering from this disease. When we exercise regularly, the following changes are likely to occur: Resting pulse rate is lowered, our blood stream develops a higher concentration of "good" cholesterol (high-density lipoproteins), we tend to eat better, and we lose weight. Scientists at the 1988 international conference concluded that these correlates of regular exercise can help us reduce the risks of atherosclerosis.

Coronary Heart Disease. Coronary heart disease is the leading cause of death in America, according to a 1990 report by the American Heart Association. This year 1.5 million Americans will have heart attacks, and more than 500,000 of them will die. It has long been argued that physical exercise can help prevent heart disease. Evidence summarized at the 1988 international conference showed how. The heart is a muscle and, like any other muscle, it becomes stronger with exercise. Just as your arm muscles get bigger when you do push-ups, the walls of your heart grow thicker with regular physical exertion. This enables it to pump more blood through the arteries with each stroke. The net result is that your heart becomes more efficient, pumping fewer times to produce the same net result. Reducing your heart rate by just one beat per minute translates into 525,600 fewer beats per year. That's impressive!

An added benefit of a stronger heart is that it can withstand stress better. Imagine you are driving and another car cuts you off. Your body goes into emergency operation, with your heart pumping rapidly to fuel your reaction to the potential crisis. Luckily your quick response averts an accident, but if your heart isn't in shape, it will continue beating rapidly long after the emergency has passed. A heart strengthened by exercise resumes its normal rhythm much sooner.

High Blood Pressure. Another benefit of exercise is especially relevant to those who suffer from hypertension. Current estimates by the American Heart Association suggest that an estimated 61 million Americans are threatened by this "silent killer," named from the fact that its victims may be unaware of any warning symptoms.

When you have your blood pressure assessed, you are given two numbers, for example, 120/80, measured on a scale of millimeters of mercury (mmHg). The first number refers to your systolic blood pressure, or the maximum pressure exerted within the artery when the heart is contracting and forcing blood out into the arterial blood vessels. The second number is the diastolic blood pressure, or the pressure in the arteries when the heart is relaxed. High blood pressure in adults is defined as a systolic pressure of 140 mmHg or greater and/or a diastolic pressure of 90 mmHg or more. Research has demonstrated that a regular program of exercise can lower resting blood pressure by about 10 millimeters of mercury. This kind of benefit can change one's diagnosis from "hypertensive" to "normal," or at least reduce the severity of this disease. Interestingly, moderate exercise such as walking may be as beneficial as more intense exercise to people considered "borderline." This is particularly important for older individuals or people suffering from orthopedic problems.

Pulmonary Disease.   When someone suffers from asthma or another lung disorder, aerobic exercise would seem to be the last thing the person would be capable of doing. Yet research summarized at the 1988 international conference argues for the benefits of exercise to asthmatics and other pulmonary patients. A medically supervised exercise program can actually lessen the disability and handicap suffered by pulmonary patients. And studies also show that, rather than being limited in their athletic abilities, asthmatics can improve their exercise performance with the help of an aerobic training program.

Osteoarthritis.   Wear and tear is part of the aging process, and it is almost universally evident in X-rays of people over age 50, where we see degenerative changes in cartilage of the joints. The underlying process of osteoarthritis is a thinning and eventual disappearance of the cartilage that forms the smooth, gliding surface of the joints. When the cartilage is worn away, bone rubs on bone, causing pain and discomfort. Some exercise might aggravate this condition, but conference reports suggested that moderate, non-weight-bearing activity, like swimming, can be quite beneficial in the treatment of arthritis and in the alleviation of some of its symptoms. According to a 1986 article in the *Journal of the American Medical Association*, even running could be an acceptable activity, despite earlier concerns that regular running programs might promote the disease.

Osteoporosis.   This condition of abnormal porousness, or "thinning," of bones tends to occur as we age, and in women more so than in men. There is strong evidence that a high level of physical activity reduces age-related bone loss. For osteoporotic patients, physical activity is considered important both for prevention and for rehabilitation.

Back Pain.   An estimated 75 million Americans suffer from chronic back pain that, according to the experts, can be prevented or ameliorated through proper exercise. In fact, an inactive lifestyle may actually contribute to the development of back problems or may aggravate the condition. Physiotherapy and physical activity are often the preferred ways of dealing with back problems over treatments involving immobilization or anti-inflammatory medications.

Cancer.   An unexpected finding in Dr. Ralph Paffenbarger's studies of the medical histories of sedentary versus active people was a lower rate of certain forms of cancer in the active group. The reasons are not entirely clear, but there is growing evidence that regular exercise can play an important role in the prevention of cancers, notably cancer of the colon.

Recovery From Surgery.   With rising medical costs and the health risks accompanying prolonged hospitalization, it is good to know that if you must undergo surgery, fitness training can reduce your recuperative time and the degree of your disability following surgery.

The Psychological Side

Evidence from the fields of psychology and psychiatry is equally compelling. Since skeptics like Dr. Henry Solomon, author of *The Exercise Myth*, argue that we get enough exercise through normal activities without taking on fitness rituals, the psychological side of the coin becomes more pertinent—and, in fact, holds great promise for helping us manage the emotional agenda of modern life. Claims of exercise benefits to psychological status range from improvements in memory and other intellectual functions to a happier and more harmonious sex life.

What most mental health professionals seem to agree on, however, is a limited but nonetheless impressive list of outcomes from the exercise habit. A National Institute of Mental Health (NIMH) panel of psychological experts recently concluded that regular exercise benefits us in the following ways.

Mental Health.   You may think of it as a feeling of well-being. Psychologists call it mental health, and research clearly shows that people who are physically fit are likely to be mentally fit as well. Regular exercisers generally score higher on measures of personal adjustment and life satisfaction.

Stress.   Stress is experienced in various bodily and mental feelings. You may feel anxious or worried. Your heart may race, and your body may feel tense. Exercise is considered to be our most dependable and least costly stress antidote. Regular exercise helps reduce temporary feelings of anxiety. It can also relieve feelings of bodily tension and lower your resting heart rate. It provides a much needed "time-out" from your daily hassles and pressing life concerns.

Depression.   You may feel "blue" for lots of reasons and for varying lengths of time. Experts identify depression as a common symptom of failure to cope with mental stress. How can exercise help? It has been shown that exercise operates on biochemical as well as psychological levels to make us feel better when we suffer the symptoms of mild to moderate depression. Studies also suggest that exercise can have benefits equal to those of short-term psychotherapy.

Anxiety.   Anxiety shows itself in mental worry and bodily sensations of tension, muscle aches, nervous stomach, and sweating. You may only feel anxious once in a while, or you may suffer from chronic anxiety. When you engage in an aerobic exercise like running or swimming, your anxiety seems to magically disappear. But it's not magic. There are solid physiological explanations for the anxiety-reducing effects of exercise. The benefits may only last for a matter of hours, but the effect is reliable enough for you to know exactly how you can relieve yourself of those tense and anxious feelings. Some studies have even shown that if you are chronically anxious, that is, you suffer from anxiety much of the time, exercise can transform you into a more relaxed person.

Self-Esteem.   At the root of most psychological discomfort is a feeling of low self-esteem. Roughly translated, this means we don't like ourselves. You might ask how exercise can help with this feeling. Exercise psychologists Robert Sonstroem and William Morgan believe the self-esteem change comes through improvements in your physical competence and a greater acceptance of your body. It might also be due to the fact that you've finally decided to do something just for yourself. Whatever the cause, there's a clear link between regular exercise and higher self-esteem. It's not the whole answer, but exercise seems to provide a reliable ego boost that may turn around a temporary crisis of confidence or a more pernicious self-attitude.

So Why Doesn't Everybody Exercise?

I have merely highlighted some of the more prominent benefits of exercise. Researchers are continuing to discover additional mental and physical rewards of the exercise habit. We will investigate these additional benefits in upcoming chapters. For now, make note of any exercise benefits that are particularly relevant to you. Know that you can count on feeling better about yourself and being healthier if you take on an exercise commitment. And then ask yourself, "If all of this is true, why don't more people exercise on a regular basis?"

If you tried to explain why people smoke, given all the evidence connecting smoking and cancer, or why people overeat, become substance abusers, or engage in unsafe sex, you would probably have a few of the reasons why people don't exercise. Let's sample some of them:

- **Hedonism:** "I like my creature comforts—no pain for me, not even good pain. And everyone knows exercise is joyless, no fun, and *hurts*."
- **Omnipotence:** "I just know that whatever bad that will happen in this life will always happen to the other guy. I have a special exemption from all the diseases and plagues of our time."
- **Rationalization:** "My heart has only so many heartbeats before it gives out. If you think I'm going to waste them on exercise, you're crazy." (Or other variations on the theme "The experts are dead wrong!")
- **Avoidance:** "There are better things to do with my time—like reading a book, watching TV, or having a little social drink with my gang."
- **Denial:** (Version 1) "My body was in shape when I was a kid, and it will always be in shape. So what if I'm 50 pounds heavier and huff and puff walking up a flight of stairs?"

   (Version 2) "I don't have to exercise to look young and attractive! Whatever I need to keep my looks, I can buy at the pharmacy or get through cosmetic surgery."

- **Superiority:** "It's beneath me to sweat, grunt, or gyrate in an aerobics class or any other kind of exercise session."
- **Inferiority:** "No matter what I try, no matter how long I work at it, I will never (a) be good at athletics, (b) look like Elle McPherson, (c) have a backhand like John McEnroe, or (d) get through a workout session without passing out. [Pick one of these or make up your own.] So why bother!"
- **Fear of Feeling:** "Exercise makes me *feel*. I don't want to get too emotionally aroused—that could be dangerous!"
- **Peer Pressure:** "People I know don't exercise! My friends would desert me if I suddenly got interested in health. They would think I was getting weird."
- **Embarrassment:** "I would look ridiculous in a leotard. I have to be in shape to even go into one of those places." (Or other variations on the theme of "People would look at me and laugh.")

If You Need an Excuse, You Can Find One!

Maybe you feel you have a valid reason not to exercise. Perhaps none of these examples accurately describes your situation. We will look at this possibility in more detail in the upcoming chapters. Right now, some of you may have caught a glimpse of yourselves. Even if you are a regular exerciser, you might still identify with one of the reasons listed above.

There are others as well, but these are simply meant to call the game for what it is—a way of not giving yourself what you need.

To illustrate the game quality of some of our excuses, a 1989 survey conducted by the National Sporting Goods Association comparing inactive Americans (those who participate in fitness activities fewer than 25 days a year) with active Americans (those participating in fitness more than 150 days a year) found virtually no difference in the amounts of free time reported by the two groups. Yet the major reason given by the inactive group for not exercising more was "lack of time"!

How Much Is Enough?

Regardless of any real or imagined limitations, you need to exercise regularly. Your body requires it—and so does your mind. However, the exact amount you need is a hotly debated subject. A consensus of experts from the American College of Sports Medicine advocates a minimum of three 20- to 30-minute exercise periods per week or, put another way, 30 minutes every other day. I refer to this as the "3 × 30" formula. Even though the calculation of time you need to exercise also depends on how intense your workout is, this formula has become a generally accepted guideline for determining whether you are getting enough exercise to reap health benefits.

What if you exercise less than three 30-minute sessions a week? Does it do any good? New evidence about exercise scheduling indicates that something is clearly better than nothing. One study at Stanford University showed that 10-minute exercise periods, if done often enough, can be of significant benefit to health and weight control. As exercise scientists broaden the definitions of exercise and the amounts needed, you may discover you are already on your way to developing the exercise habit.

Exercise guidelines like the "3 × 30" formula can be misleading. On the one hand, if you don't exercise this amount, you may give up on exercise altogether believing it isn't enough. On the other hand, if you do more than that amount, you may be considered fanatical.

The fact is that some people haven't even begun to "exercise" at the end of 30 minutes—that's just their warm-up. Others are spent in half that time. A popular rule of thumb among exercise scientists is that people who exercise more than about 2 hours a day are considered to be verging on addiction in the most negative sense of the word, although thousands of well-adjusted, intelligent, and even busy people exercise that much or more every day.

Dr. Ken Cooper, reigning guru of the aerobics movement, has changed his thinking on this matter. He used to think it didn't matter how much you exercised. Gauging amounts by miles run, Dr. Cooper now believes that if you run more than about 15 miles per week (which roughly translates into 3 hours of exercise), you are doing it for something other than fitness.

Researchers at Cooper's Institute for Aerobics Research in Dallas seem to be moving farther and farther away from the "3 × 30" formula. Steven Blair, director of epidemiology at Cooper's Institute, says it's wrong to define exercise according to something like the 3 × 30 rule. Speaking from solid research, he concludes, "A little bit of exercise is better than being totally sedentary. . . . You don't have to get out there and be an athlete, but escape from the bottom group of the 20% of people who are truly sedentary." According to Blair, most people would probably say, "I can do that." Precisely so! Your body requires exercise, but there is no need to train for a marathon, take daily aerobics classes, or pump iron so you look like Arnold Schwarzenegger.

What's the right amount for you? Consider an analogy from the field of nutrition. An expert committee appointed by the National Academy of Sciences has established Recommended Dietary Allowances (RDAs) for vitamins, minerals, proteins, fats, and carbohydrates. These minimum standards do not, however, address the particular needs you may have. They are general, conservative, baseline figures. Depending on your age, sex, lifestyle, and body composition, you may need to modify your intake for reasons of physical health and emotional well-being. And of course, you always have to bear in mind the problem of toxic doses! The same principle applies to determining the right exercise prescription for your mental and physical needs. As you read on, you will come to better understand your needs and how they dictate what the best exercise plan is for you to reach your personal objectives.

Actions Speak Louder Than Words

As a last step before examining what can motivate you to exercise, let's take a closer look at our current state of fitness. The evidence is impressive. It tells us no matter how much we talk about fitness, no matter how much money we spend on athletic pursuits, and no matter how much we bow to advice from the media, the average citizen simply isn't exercising enough to attain minimal standards for health maintenance. Modern fitness is mostly "smoke and mirrors." Living an active lifestyle in the '90s may have more to do with buying activewear than being active. We spend close to $46 billion on fitness, yet a 1990 U.S. Public Health Service report estimates that no more than 1 in 10 Americans (about 10%) gets sufficient exercise to benefit heart and lungs. Some other estimates show as high as 20% to 30% of the adult population as active, but that still leaves a majority who are either marginally active or inactive. We may

"THE 11TH COMMANDMENT: THOU SHALT EXERCISE!"

get some exercise in the form of housework, gardening, or walking to the bus, but most of us could use more in the way of aerobic workouts.

According to a 1989 report, the sorry state of our physical fitness applies not only to the adult population, but also to the condition of our youth. A 10-year study by the Chrysler Fund—Amateur Athletic Union testing program shows that children ages 6 to 17 demonstrate some increase in muscular strength, but have also gained weight and lost cardiovascular endurance, since 1980. The findings were described as "ominous" by Dr. Wynn Updyke, director of the testing program, because of the clear link between heart disease and obesity and inactivity.

About 9.7 million children participated in the testing; results showed, among other things, a decrease from 43% to 32% since 1980 of kids rating "satisfactory" on the entire test, an approximately 60-second increase in girls' running time for the mile race to an average in the 9- to 10-minute range, and a 14-pound increase in boys' weight since 1983.

If our children are becoming less fit, there is real concern for the future. Statistics show that the older we are, the less active we become. In a three-category rating—"active," "less active," and "inactive,"—73% of the over-65 age group fell into the "inactive" category, whereas only 54% of the 25- to 34-year-old group was classified this way. Whether you are male or female, on the other hand, makes little difference. Adult men and women exercise to about the same degree.

In other respects, the exercising public seems to be a little more affluent and to have attained a higher level of education than those who maintain an inactive lifestyle, but not enough to say that education and money are what you need to exercise. It's more complicated than that. Exercisers are more health conscious, smoke less, watch less television, and generally feel healthier than nonexercisers. The predominant explanation for these findings is that when you start an exercise program, you become more concerned about how you feel, what you do with your time, and how you look.

There is good reason to be hopeful about people who currently don't exercise. Of the more than 90 million adult Americans estimated by the National Sporting Goods Association to be physically inactive "couch potatoes," 57% say they want to do more. The problem is described as a lack of motivation by over 51% of inactive Americans.

To motivate yourself, you have to want something enough to go after it day after day, week after week. That's why this book is so important. It will help you find your motivation, identify your goals, and counter your resistance.

How Can You Get Going?

How can you turn yourself on to exercise? And how do you keep your commitment going? The answer lies in finding your motivational hooks for developing the exercise habit. You may think it's obvious, but it's not. You may say, "I know I have to lose 10 pounds, and that's why I should exercise," but if you know that and you're not exercising, why aren't you? The answer is that weight loss is only one of your motivations, and it may be insufficient to get you over all the hurdles on the road to developing an exercise habit. You need to assess *all your motives* and see how they combine to create your ideal exercise plan—a plan that is unique to your needs, not merely one that happens to be in vogue, and not necessarily the one that is most convenient.

You have to look at all the angles of your personality and appreciate how the right exercise plan can satisfy your deepest life motives. It's possible. Give yourself a real chance. Go through the personal assessments in Part II and get to know what's important to you. Find out how the word *exercise* expands into a spectrum of possibilities for personal growth and fulfillment. If exercise conjures up images of drudgery or heavy-footed joggers, erase them. Empty your mind of definitions of what exercise is until you discover its personal meaning for your life.

CHAPTER 2

THE WIDE WORLD OF EXERCISE MOTIVATION

"The only reason I would take up jogging is to hear heavy breathing again."
ERMA BOMBECK

What's Exercise Motivation?

Exercise motivation—some say you have to be born with it, others say you can acquire it, and then there are those who think you have it because of what it gives you. Sound confusing? Well, it may be now, but by the time you finish this book, you not only will understand it but will also be able to use it in developing your exercise habit.

Think of it as a reason to exercise. One person may not know why she exercises—she always has and says she always will. We may call her a born athlete! Another says he hated sports growing up, but now has come to enjoy them. We may refer to his as an acquired interest. Then there's the person who wants to lose weight, develop some muscles, or stay healthy. We say this person has extrinsic motives, wanting something that results from athletic participation.

Where Do You Fit?

You may be trying to figure out where you fit. Do you have an innate interest in exercise? Have you come to enjoy sports over the years? Or are you interested because of what exercise can do for you? Strangely enough, you should be able to answer "yes" to each of these questions.

Let's start at the beginning. As infants, we all enjoyed crawling, climbing, tumbling, walking, running, and so many other variations of movement that our parents may have run out of paper listing the new things we did each day. Years passed, and we moved along different paths. Some of us continued to run and tumble; others became more sedentary. Why we changed can only be known through studying our personal histories, but one thing seems certain: We all started out enjoying our bodies in movement—and that's about as good a definition of exercise as we need right now.

The second question was whether our interest in sports and exercise developed over the years. As our crawling-tumbling-running movements were shaped by eager parents or teachers into specialized exercises, we may have found strong reasons to disengage from activity. We may have gotten hurt; other kids may have picked on us; or perhaps there was too much pressure on us to perform. Later on, when the pressures were removed, the bullies went away, and we learned how to avoid getting hurt, we may have reconnected with sport and exercise. If we didn't, perhaps that was because we no longer believed we could, or we hadn't done it in so long that we thought we didn't want to.

If your original answer was "no" to the question of whether you acquired an interest in sport and exercise, I would like you to change it to "not yet," because by the time you have finished this book, I believe you will have rediscovered your connection to physical movement.

The third question was whether you exercise for extrinsic motives. Here, I know we can all answer "yes," because even if you love playing sports and working out, the benefits derived from participation far exceed the simple pleasures of these games and pastimes. I am referring to the kinds of benefits to health and psychological well-being discussed in chapter 1.

So, the essential point here is that everyone has the motivation to exercise. It may be covered over by decades of suppression or accumulated fears about physical activity. Disuse may have eroded some of your talent and also made it difficult for your muscles to cooperate on those inspired occasions when your mind agrees to exercise. With current images of what an athletic person *should* look like, you may feel quite alienated from anything that resembles sport because you think you don't belong. If this is the case, you need to change your thinking by discovering the wide world of exercise motivations inside you.

From Childhood to Now

Simple childhood pleasures get transformed over the years so that your adult motivations represent a more complex mix of wants and needs. This applies equally well to the motivation to exercise. For this reason, it's important to pause before delving into your more complex adult nature and reflect on the primal joy you felt in your body as an infant and child. You need to remind yourself that, in those early years, you weren't at all self-conscious about how you looked or whether you were doing it right. You moved and played because you wanted to and because it felt good.

Imagine the expressions on a toddler's face as she takes her first solo steps—doubt, fear, anticipation that suddenly bursts into ecstasy as she realizes she is walking on her own. No one told her this would be fun. She knew it instinctively. Where did this knowledge go? Believe it or not, you still have it deep inside. The experiences of growing up may stifle or thwart it, but with some careful nurturing you can bring it back. That's what this book is about—helping you connect not only with your grown-up motives for exercising but with those primitive pleasures that came from the free expressions of your body.

Is an Exercise Motive More Than a Reason?

If you look up the word *motive* in psychological manuals, you can find dozens of definitions. After simplifying the jargon, what you are left with are two sides to a motive, like the flip sides of a coin. One side says a motive is a push that moves you toward some goal or object. The implication is that the push comes from inside. An example is hunger. You feel the pangs in your stomach, and you go in search of food. Hunger motivates you to find food. It pushes you.

The other side says a motive is a pull that draws you toward the goal or object. The implication here is that the pull comes from outside. If you stay with the example of hunger, you might imagine some absolutely scrumptious dessert like hot apple pie with vanilla ice cream or an exquisitely prepared meal that makes you drool. Like a magnet, the food arouses your hunger and draws you to it. It pulls you.

I used the example of hunger because it clarifies how both sides of the definition have to be taken into account. Like the magnet that pulls you, there has to be something of a certain makeup inside you to respond. Magnets won't attract wood or paper, but they will draw little metal balls.

You may feel that some of your motives are strictly pushes and others are pulls. That is, you experience some of the things that motivate you as being outside of you, while others you believe are within. Money may motivate you, and money is something outside your skin. But if you ask, "What is it about money that I want?" the answer usually comes down to something inside of you, like self-esteem or pride. This is just another way of referring back to the magnet and the little metal ball. What may be most obvious is the power of the magnet, because of how it pulls things toward it, but the objects pulled by the magnet have to be of a certain chemical structure. If not, the magnet is powerless. It's an interaction of two things, where both sides are necessary.

Whether you think of your motivations as internal pushes that make you do things or external magnets that draw you, in a commonsense way you are likely to talk about motives as your reasons for doing things. The fine details of whether a motive feels more like a push or a pull, something outside or inside, a goal that is real or imaginary, are what give character to different motives.

Any technical discussion of what a motive is ultimately translates into an experience you have of wanting something. When that *want* becomes strong, you may call it a *need*. If asked to explain why you did something or why you are pursuing a particular goal, you offer your reasons. These are simply the different ways we talk about motives.

Throughout this book, we will take a practical perspective on motives, describing them as things that push you or pull you, as needs and wants, and as reasons for doing things—especially for exercising. Let's move from this abstract discussion of motives to a more concrete one where you can see where your exercise motivation originates.

Are There Different Types of Exercise Motives?

Psychologists have come up with a long list of human motives. What motivates us to exercise, however, represents only part of that list. For example, you may feel a certain economic motivation—a desire to have sufficient money to cover your expenses and provide a comfortable standard of living. Can an economic motive make you want to exercise? It can, if you are planning a career as a professional athlete. Otherwise, money is not likely to be a relevant exercise motive.

Identifying the Relevant Motives: The Three Types

A good way to determine what motives are relevant to exercise is to ask yourself some fundamental questions about what exercise means to you. Whether or not you presently exercise, you might recognize the potential exercise holds to shape your body. This could mean losing weight or building muscles. You should also realize how it's good for your health. These *body motives*, as we will call them, are what most people discuss when answering questions about what motivates them to exercise, but there are also two other types of motives.

Psychological motives may not be why people start exercising, but often they are the reasons people continue. You may commence an exercise program to lose weight but through your fitness experiences learn how helpful exercise can be to reducing mental and physical tensions or to improving your mood.

Social motives come out of your interests in people and the ways in which you prefer to relate to others. Whether you like to be alone or with others, whether or not you enjoy competition, or how well you express your needs to others represent aspects of your social nature—and motives for exercising. If, for example, you enjoy competition, think of all the opportunities exercise presents for you to satisfy this desire.

For the most part, your motivations to exercise will derive from either something relating to your body, a psychological concern, or a social interest. In fact, you are likely to find that your reasons to exercise come from all three types of motives. How much you are motivated by each type is what you will be examining in the upcoming chapters. Knowing where your motivations are based will help you choose the right exercise plan and continue with it to develop a healthy exercise habit.

Measuring Your Motives

Part II of this book presents quizzes to measure your exercise motives. These Fitness Incentives Quizzes cover a total of 18 different motives that will help connect your body and mind to the right exercise plan. The quizzes are divided into three types: body, psychological, and social motives. Specific instructions are provided with the quizzes, but a few aspects of the quizzes require a more general explanation.

Completing the Fitness Incentives Quizzes

Questions in the Fitness Incentives Quizzes are straightforward. There are no trick answers. What's required is your thoughtfulness and an honest self-appraisal. We need to consider first how you should answer the questions and then how you will score your quizzes.

Answering the Questions.   To illustrate how to answer the questions, we will use two examples showing the different kinds of responses required. Here's the first:

SAMPLE QUESTION # 1

Whenever I am in a car, I wear a seatbelt.

There are three possible answers:

Y = Yes   N = No   I = In between

Even if you think you know how to answer, consider the following explanation so there is no confusion. A "yes" answer means that almost every time you get into a car, in the front seat or the back, as driver or passenger, you fasten your seatbelt. A "no" answer means you just about never put on your seatbelt. What does "in between" mean? In this case, it means you wear your seatbelt less than always and more than never. Maybe you wear it whenever you ride in the front of the car, but not when you are in the back seat. Most cars have seatbelts in the back seat, so you would have to answer "in between" if you don't use a belt when one is available.

What if you have been in a car that didn't have seatbelts and that's the only time you didn't wear one? You would answer "yes" because your intention is to always wear a seatbelt; whenever you didn't, it was because you couldn't, not because you didn't try to wear one.

What if you never travel in cars? In this case, you will have to imagine what you would do. Do you think you would wear a seatbelt? If you think so, you would answer "yes." If you believe you definitely wouldn't, you would answer "no." If you are uncertain or think it might depend on the situation, you would answer "in between." This sample question has the potential of being answered with a clear yes or no response. Occasionally, the quiz questions will be less black and white, so you will have to reflect a little longer on your answer. Consider the following example:

SAMPLE QUESTION # 2

I like the way my body looks.

Once again, there are three possible answers:

Y = Yes   N = No   I = In between

There aren't too many people who always feel good about the way their bodies look. Most of us go up and down, hovering around a more or less positive or negative attitude toward our bodies. So how are you supposed to answer?

If you generally like the way your body looks, you would answer "yes." This means on most days and in an overall sense, you like your body. You may not like your nose or your feet too much, but you feel pretty okay about the total package.

A "no" answer means you generally dislike the way your body looks. It doesn't have to be as strong as disgust or hatred, but your overall attitude toward many parts of your body or your body as a whole is one of dissatisfaction.

"In between" can mean a number of things. It might mean you are in conflict—in a love-hate relationship, where sometimes you feel great and other times you feel lousy about your body. It balances out somewhere in the middle. Or it might mean that you feel your body is mediocre—not bad and not good, just average. You don't like it, and you don't dislike it.

What if you have never thought about whether you like your body? Well, now's the time to do it. Conjure up a mental image of your body and see how you feel about it. Or take a good look at your body in a full-length mirror, and notice your emotional response. Do you like what you see, or not? Depending on your reaction, you can now answer the question "yes," "no," or somewhere "in between." A general rule for questions you haven't thought about or don't know how to answer is to find out now. You may need to delve into your thoughts or ask friends for feedback about how they perceive you. *Don't use the "in between" answer as a way of saying "I don't know"!* Give each question full consideration. A little effort will provide the answer you are looking for.

Scoring the Quizzes.   Your answers have to be converted to a point system to obtain your scores. The way to do this is follow the instructions accompanying each of the quizzes.

The scoring procedure will be as follows:

- 2 points for a "yes"
- 1 point for an "in between"
- 0 points for a "no"

Five questions will be used to assess each of your motives. This means that, in scoring each quiz, you will add up the corresponding point values for your answers on five questions. You can obtain a maximum score of 10 if you answer all questions with a "yes" (5 questions × 2 points each = 10 points). If you answer all five questions "no," your score would be zero (5 questions × 0 points each = 0 points). In all likelihood, you will answer some questions "yes," some "no," and some "in between," resulting in a score between 0 and 10 points. The next thing you want to know is what these numbers mean.

What Your Scores Mean

There are two parts to understanding your scores. The first has to do with the interpretation of the number itself. That is, when does your score mean that you have high motivation and when does it mean your motivation is low? The second has to do with any value judgments you might be inclined to make as a result of your score. For example, does your score mean that you are healthy or unhealthy, happy or sad, and so forth.

The Numerical Meaning

The numerical interpretation is easy, and to make sure it remains that way, you will be reminded of it each time you are asked to interpret your score in Part II. Here's the system:

If your score is from . . .	Your motivation is considered . . .
0 to 3	Low
4 to 6	Moderate
7 to 10	High

That's all there is to it. You will become familiar with the numbering system as you use it, but for now let's move on to a more central consideration—what value you attach to your scores.

Judging Your Scores

The numerical explanation tells you that the higher your score is on a particular quiz, the more it serves to motivate your behavior. So, a high score means you have identified something that motivates you; a low score means the opposite—the motive in question won't spur you to exercise.

This is not the same as saying "High scores are good and low scores are bad." Whatever your score is, there is no criticism inherent in the scoring system about who you are or how you approach life. The judgment is left to you—but it's essential that you look at all your scores in a positive light.

Many people begin an exercise program because they feel dissatisfied with themselves. When you obtain a test score that can be interpreted in a negative light, it can form another basis for self-rejection. For example, if your score on the Self-Esteem Quiz shows you have ambivalent feelings about your self-worth, you might be inclined to make statements like "See! I knew I wasn't any good." Adding self-blame to your analysis only increases the burden at the beginning of developing an exercise habit.

One of the most profound views we can express as we work on ourselves in the exercise realm is one of self-acceptance. Commenting in the *Kripalu Yoga Quest*, Yogi Amrit Desai offers inspired guidance for fitness beginners: "We need a high level of energy and enthusiasm if we are to take constructive actions toward changing our lives. When we accept ourselves as we are today and gradually proceed to make the changes we want for ourselves, we have more power to recreate our lives. When we are self-accepting, we love ourselves for not being perfect already. The burden of self-rejection makes it very hard to change our lives."

If you obtain a score that makes you feel uneasy, you will also have opportunities of deciding how to redirect your focus. There are 18 motives in the Fitness Incentives Quizzes—you can choose new ways of motivating yourself instead of relying on motives you may question at this point in your life.

Read carefully each motive's explanation to appreciate how it should be interpreted and how it can work for you. As a quick example, a high score on the Weight Worry Quiz does not mean you manage your weight well or that you are able to keep your weight at the right level. To the contrary, it means you are struggling with weight problems or that you are obsessed with worries of weight control. Consequently, you are likely to be motivated to do things that will help you manage your weight better—and exercise is certainly one of the best methods available.

You may say, "So what? I already knew that!" However, what you may not be aware of are the kinds of exercise programs that will work best for you. Or you may not know how much time you will have to invest to achieve the results you seek. This is where *The Exercise Habit* will help you. And for motives that are more indirectly connected to exercise, learning how you can fuel a positive exercise habit with these deeper motives will be invaluable.

On Your Mark, Get Set . . .

Sharpen your pencil, clear your mind, and let your fingers turn the pages. It's time to jump in—to leave the sidelines of this approaching self-analysis and begin the search for your motives and your exercise match.

There are two main ways of completing Part II. The first is to complete all the quizzes in Part II and then go back to read about their interpretations. The second is to take it a step at a time, completing one quiz and reading its interpretation before going on to the next. Both ways are fine, but it's not recommended to let too long a period elapse between your beginning the quizzes in Part II and completing them. You want to have the same mental set when you are taking the quizzes. If you let too much time pass, you may alter your approach to the quizzes and affect the comparisons you can make between your motives.

The quizzes are clearly marked in Part II. There are 18 of them, and you should be able to complete them all in about 1 hour or less. If you choose to do them altogether, allow yourself this much time. If you choose to do them separately, plan to complete Part II of this book within a period of 2 to 3 weeks. Letting it take more than this amount of time could affect the validity of comparisons among your quiz scores.

When you finish the quizzes in Part II, you will move through some of the more practical steps of identifying the right exercise plan and fitting it into your schedule. Part III will highlight obstacles you may encounter and advise you of ways around them. It will also take you through a final "attitude check" to make sure your mind has the right perspective about your exercise commitment.

On your mark, get set, . . . go!

P·A·R·T · II

THE FITNESS INCENTIVES QUIZZES— AND WHAT THEY MEAN TO YOU

CHAPTER 3

YOUR BODY MOTIVES
AND HOW TO USE THEM

"To keep the body in good health is a duty . . . otherwise we shall not be able to
keep our mind strong and clean."
BUDDHA

Do you

- always need to look good in order to feel good?
- want to feel more sexually alive?
- have trouble getting your addictions under control?
- obsess about your weight or feeling fat?
- worry about your health and the possibilities of disease?
- strive to be youthful for as long as you live?

If you answered "yes" to any of these questions, your life motivations
are intricately related to your body.

What Are Your Body Motives?

Most people who exercise say they do it for physical reasons, notably
health, weight, or keeping fit. There are other motives relating to our
bodies that can also help us develop the exercise habit. These include
concerns about how we look, the enjoyment of sexual energy, and the
desire to feel young and stave off signs of aging.

Another less obvious body motive derives from our need to get negative
addictions under control. Drugs and alcohol are common addictions, food
in excess also qualifies, and recent studies label some sexual patterns as
addictive problems. People with these addictions may be able to replace
the negative addiction with a positive exercise habit.

How do you rate on these motives? How can they help you develop a healthy, lifelong exercise habit? You must first take a quiz on each motive to obtain your score. Then you will learn how that motive relates to exercise and how to interpret your score.

—————————————— **Vanity Quiz** ——————————————

Answer Each Question YES, NO, or IN BETWEEN
(Y = Yes   N = No   I = In between)

_____ 1. I am extremely conscious of my physical appearance.

_____ 2. My emotions go up or down depending on how good I look.

_____ 3. Whenever I pass a mirror or store window, I look at myself.

_____ 4. I am aware of every imperfection in my physical appearance.

_____ 5. Even when I am running errands, I make sure I look as good as I can.

Scoring: Give yourself 2 points for "yes" answers, 1 point for "in between" answers, and 0 points for "no" answers. Total your points for questions 1 through 5.

Your score = _____ (0 to 10 points)

What's Your V.Q. (Vanity Quotient)?

The myth of Narcissus is about a young man who fell in love with his reflection in a pool of water and subsequently drowned pursuing it. Psychologists tell us that a modest degree of narcissism is healthy and normal, but in excess it interferes with our interpersonal relationships. Vanity is connected to narcissism, being defined as an "inflated pride in one's appearance." At one extreme, when a person fails to take pride in his or her appearance, we attach labels of low self-worth, depression, or slovenliness. At the other extreme, when someone is overly concerned with looking good, we attach labels of vanity or narcissism.

Even though psychologists favor a moderate degree of vanity over the extremes, we have to be careful about taking a critical or judgmental attitude. All of our motivations derive from experiences in our lives. We are who we are for good reasons. Self-acceptance is absolutely essential to personal development. So, we start from the position that any score on the Vanity Quiz is a good place to begin.

Having pride in your body and wanting to look good is strongly encouraged by our culture. You might even say we exalt the body and its potential beauty. Talented people who are beautiful make the covers of popular magazines. Talented, not-so-beautiful people get essays written about them—or, if we do see their pictures, it's only after makeup artists have performed a masterful coverup. As a Camay soap ad from the 1930s put it, "Life is a beauty contest!"

Would you believe that even people who seem totally unconcerned with their appearance have deep-seated insecurities about their looks? Sociologist Dr. Barry Glassner says we are tyrannized by the quest for bodily perfection. In his book *Bodies: Why We Look the Way We Do (And How We Feel About It)*, Glassner unmasks the narcissism in our culture. He doesn't think it is rooted in personality so much as prompted by business interests. He notes that Americans spend over $50 billion a year on plastic surgery, cosmetics, diets, health clubs, and related beauty pursuits. We are encouraged at every turn to feed our vanity, to play into the impossible dream of remaining forever beautiful.

Sara Tucker, writing in *Shape* magazine on "the ideal body," believes the problem is more complex for women. "Beauty is power, as well as part of the definition of femininity. It is seen as a woman's *business* to be beautiful. . . . Nowadays, the test of a woman's beauty is what she sees when she stands naked in front of her bathroom mirror. We've stripped fashion down to the basics: the beautiful body is what it's all about." Roberta Pollack Seid, author of *Never Too Thin*, thinks our preoccupation

"IS BEAUTY ONLY SKIN DEEP?"

with physical appearance stems partly from the mobility of modern life, the fact that we are continually making "first impressions." In previous generations, people lived and died in communities where they were born. Appearance still counted, but it was judged in the context of other qualities the person possessed. People were known more by their characters, by the enduring qualities of their personalities.

Dr. Seid believes the breakdown of family and other social structures that once provided security has deprived us of an inner self-confidence. In our search for approval, we've turned to fashion with a kind of religious zeal. "In a secular age," says Seid, "it becomes much more important to manipulate your appearance rather than your soul or your ethics." Ultimately, each person must seek a balance, a point of healthy narcissism. You may decry the sociocultural blackmail to maintain beauty, but if you obsess about your physical appearance, you have no choice other than to accept where you are and work with your needs—at least until you experience a change in your values.

Interpreting Your Score

If you score high on the Vanity Quiz, treat vanity as an important aspect of your personality and use it to your advantage. Scores are considered high when your total is 7 or more and low when they are 3 or less. Scores of 4, 5, and 6 are considered moderate.

So what does it mean if you have a high score on vanity? There are two possible interpretations. A high score could indicate that you are extremely proud of your physical qualities. You like the way you look, and you make every effort to maintain or improve your appearance. A second possibility is that you show extreme concern with your physical appearance, but you do so out of a deep-seated insecurity. Your attention to appearance derives from fears that you will never look good enough or that people will reject you based on your looks. Your preoccupation with appearance is your way of making yourself feel "okay" when you are out in the world.

If you score high on vanity, you probably know the importance of exercise for looking your best, and you may favor exercise programs that concentrate on "spot reducing" or "body shaping." You may not be as concerned about other benefits.

What if you score high and don't exercise? You may have been gifted with a body you like that until now hasn't required much maintenance work—or you go in for cosmetic solutions. Time, gravity, and Mother Nature will inevitably exact their due. And the exercise habit may be one of the few reliable aids for your vanity. Of course, choosing the right exercise is crucial.

Some high scorers may avoid exercise out of embarrassment, feeling that it's just too risky to put on a spandex outfit and walk into an aerobics studio. Knowing more about your options will help you make that needed connection to the exercise world.

If you're a high scorer, what kind of exercise program is right for you? And what should you avoid? Having a high score on vanity means you can motivate yourself by getting solid advice about exercise programs that will do for your body what your ego needs. Expose yourself to information about physical activities that focus on aspects of your body you want to improve.

Be careful to also learn about the downside of certain sports—and protect yourself accordingly. You may already know that a regular regimen of running results in sagging jowls. The skin becomes less elastic as you age. For every mile you run, your skin gets jarred and pulled nearly 2,000 times as your steps pound the body onto the earth with a force between 3 and 10 times your weight! Do speed walking instead of running—it results in less damage to the body, and, most importantly, it saves your skin from looking like it was stretched one too many times. If you do aerobics, get in the habit of choosing low-impact classes over high-impact ones, for the same reasons. Watch out for overchlorinated pools that dry skin and damage hair. Stair-climbing machines are great for developing the buttocks, but be careful not to cheat by leaning on the railings—your shoulders may end up around your ears, and when garment shoulder pads are out of style, where will that leave you? Also, make sure to shade your skin from the sun when exercising outdoors. It's not just lying on the beach that attracts the sun's wrinkling rays.

If you knew all this, that's great. But if you're not familiar with the exercise world, recognize that not all exercise is created equal, especially when it comes to shaping and toning your body.

Your motives may change over time, but if this is where your investment is right now, go for it—with intelligence. Choose carefully. An unsupervised weight-training program may create a rather odd-looking torso. Men who equate attractiveness with big "pecs" (chest muscles) and biceps (arm muscles) may look a bit strange when they expose their gangly legs at the beach. Working on muscles in the front of the torso without equal emphasis on those in back can make your body look like it belongs to a split personality. Your program has to be balanced with equal emphasis on all the body's parts.

Be realistic about your expectations. Find out how much you have to put in to get out what you want. Magazine articles that promise a "new, beautiful you—with just 5 minutes of exercise a day" will ultimately disappoint you. It takes a lot more than that. The fact is that you're not likely to achieve substantial change in body proportions with the recommended 30 minutes of exercise every other day. If you are committed to looking good, get behind your commitment with a daily exercise plan. And keep in mind that the right plan for you should be designed to address all your body's needs. You may spend 2 days a week on activities like body shaping or weight training, another 2 doing moderate aerobic workouts, and 2 more practicing stretching routines like yoga.

What does a low vanity score mean? You could have a low score because you are so convinced of your good looks that you never give it a second thought—or because you simply pay little attention to your physical appearance. This doesn't necessarily mean you are careless in your appearance; it might mean that appearance isn't a major focus of your attention. Your motivational hooks are likely to lie elsewhere.

On the other hand, extremely low scores may signal an attitude of defeat. You may have given up on ever improving your appearance. You deserve a second chance. Not only can exercise make you look better, it can help you feel better about the way you look!

In a 1985 *Psychology Today* body image survey, results revealed that people who cared about fitness and health had more positive feelings about their appearance than did people who were only concerned with their appearance. One implication of this study is that getting involved in fitness will prove your commitment to looking good and should boost your self-image as well.

Nat had always been extremely conscious of his appearance, but he hadn't worried about his weight until he realized he had gained too much to lose in a week or two of dieting. At age 44, he decided it was time to begin exercising. With some smart dieting and a three-times-a-week exercise plan, he dropped his weight from 230 to 190 pounds, but he retained his original pear shape. He was getting discouraged and resolved to consult a trainer. The trainer gave him a 6-day program with Sunday off. That was quite a commitment, but he did it. Within 6 months his body showed results. His chest went from 38 inches to 41 inches, and his waist dropped 3 inches, from 37 inches to 34 inches. Interestingly, he never complained. He could see the changes from week to week, and—after all—that was his purpose.

Sexuality Quiz

Answer Each Question YES, NO, or IN BETWEEN
(Y = Yes   N = No   I = In between)

_____ 1. I consider myself to be a sexy person.

_____ 2. Enjoying my sexuality is *essential* to my sense of well-being.

_____ 3. Having an active and satisfying sex life is one of my priorities.

_____ 4. I go to great lengths to keep myself looking and feeling sexy.

_____ 5. I like being around people who turn me on physically.

Scoring: Give yourself 2 points for "yes" answers, 1 point for "in between" answers, and 0 points for "no" answers. Total your points for questions 1 through 5.

Your score = _____ (0 to 10 points)

Where's Your Sexuality?

Sex is a basic biological drive, yet we do everything possible to divert it, distort it, channel it, inflate it, or even deny it. We worry about losing it, not getting it, or not knowing what to do with it. We live with problems of too much or too little but rarely just enough.

Something so simple gets so complex when we throw it into the blender of human emotions. Surveys of sexual practices from Kinsey to Hite tell us what's normal and what's not. We develop expectations of how often we should engage in sex, how much time to spend on foreplay, what satisfies a woman, what satisfies a man. Sexologists also tell us why we lose interest in sex or, in some cases, the ability to perform sexually.

Surveys like Morton Hunt's study of sexual behavior inform us that, if you are between 18 and 24, the norm for having sexual intercourse is close to four times per week. It drops to about twice a week in the age range of 35 to 44. After 55 sexual frequency may decline below once a week. Popular opinion says the more the better. That is, if you engage in sex on a daily basis, that's great. The problem here is when your partner isn't of a similar inclination—or worse, if you don't have a partner.

We also know that sex is far more than intercourse or orgasm. There are all those wonderful mating rituals that stir our blood and send hormones coursing through our bodies. Office flirtations, sidewalk beauty pageants, musky glances across a crowded room feed our sensual selves. We feel lustfully alive when someone notices us in that certain way. We may invite it by the way we dress or the way we walk, or through a long, languorous look.

There is the other extreme—when we are dead from the neck down, when we think and act as if we have been neutered. Somehow, somewhere we lost touch with our sexuality. Whether it was through denial, repression, or conscious sublimation, we tuned out and chose not to respond. We ran away when we heard the primal call.

What does this have to do with exercise? Part of the answer is that people who exercise regularly report a higher interest in sex than those who do not. Young women answering a survey by *Shape* magazine said they felt more easily aroused immediately after they exercised. Another study, conducted by Dr. David Frauman at Ohio University, noted that the more people exercised, the more they wanted sex, and the more they had it. Physiological analysis shows that this isn't merely a matter of attitude. Rigorous physical exercise actually increases the level of sex hormones in the bloodstream.

Linda DeVillers, a West Coast psychologist who runs workshops for women on building sexual confidence through exercise, studied 8,000 women who had been exercising aerobically at least three times a week for 3 months or more. Her results quoted in the June 1990 issue of *Longevity* magazine indicated that after the exercise regimen, 40% felt more easily aroused, 33% reported increased sexual activity, and 26% found it easier to reach climax.

In another study, masters-level swimmers in their 40s and 60s reported more active sex lives than people half their age. According to Philip Whitten and Elizabeth Whiteside, 97% of swimmers in their 40s and 92% of those in their 60s said they were sexually active—an exceptionally high rate compared to the general population. The frequency of sex among swimmers 40 and over was similar to that reported by many people in their 20s and 30s. Most interesting, the frequency of sex didn't drop off; swimmers in their 60s were almost as active as swimmers in their 40s.

Most researchers believe the exercise effect on sexuality is more than physical. It influences our energy, self-image, and interpersonal relations. Rachel Meltzer Wallace, reporting on 25 years of women's fitness in *Cosmopolitan*, sums it up: "Today, being strong and healthy is fun. We like the lift we get from working out, the feeling of accomplishment that comes with doing something physically demanding, doing it well. *It's downright sexy."*

Interpreting Your Score

What do your scores on the Sexuality Quiz mean? High scores (7 or more) indicate you enjoy your sexuality and you may even be playfully provocative. You also get turned on being around people who live in their bodies more than in their heads. You flirt, though you may opt out on the follow-through. Feeling sexy is synonymous with feeling good.

If you score high, you may be drawn to fitness activities that have sex appeal. Aerobics and dance rate high on this dimension, but other activities may have a similar effect. Runners also report increased interest in sex as a result of their workouts, according to Royce Flippin in the March 1987 issue of *The Runner*. So it doesn't have to be a high-fashion activity to titillate your libido. It may simply be the reconnection with your body through exercise that makes the difference.

There is a caution, however. The study by Whitten and Whiteside noted earlier found that people who train beyond 2 hours per day may experience a decline in sexual interest and activity. Is this the old story of too much of a good thing? Perhaps, but there are other explanations. Like anything that is potentially good for us, when taken to excess it can turn sour. This goes for things like food, work, and even exercise. The distinguishing factor may not be how much you exercise but why you are exercising. If you exercise to escape a difficult relationship, it would come as no surprise that your interest in sex has diminished. You unconsciously redirect all your energy from the bedroom to your workouts. Psychologists call this sublimation or avoidance. So, before you set limits on your exercise plan, think twice about why you are exercising. The motivational tests in this book will provide a good means of identifying your hidden needs.

What about low scores? If you scored 3 points or less, you may want to ask yourself a more fundamental question, "Am I satisfied with my sex life?" It's quite possible to have a satisfying sex life and a low score on the Sexuality Quiz. If that's you, then you will find your exercise motives elsewhere. But if you have a low score and answer "no" to this question, consider the possibility that your sexuality shuts down when you lose touch with your body. I believe even moderate exercise like walking or yoga can be of immense benefit to the mind-body connection. It is wittily said that the mind is the body's largest sexual organ. But just as a pilot needs a plane to fly, so the mind's interests must be channeled through a vitalized body. Exercise is a surefire way to reawaken your sexual spirit and put you back in touch with your body.

George had been "single again" for 5 years. He thought his marriage had simply fizzled—no passion. After a few years in the singles' scene, he realized that perhaps he owned some responsibility for the problem. Lovers seemed to drift out of his life with little explanation and even less remorse. The only thing he experienced intensely was his work. He put in 60-hour weeks as a high school principal.

Colleagues became concerned for his health and urged him to join the faculty's noontime exercise club. He saw it as part of his duty and reluctantly agreed. George had shot a few hoops in his school days, and gradually he earned a spot on the faculty basketball team. Whether it was his new star status or the reawakened competitor within, George was a changed man. He had more vitality, more sparkle in his eyes. His new girlfriend just thought he was a passionate kind of guy.

Addictive Behaviors Quiz

Answer Each Question YES, NO, or IN BETWEEN
(Y = Yes   N = No   I = In between)

_____ 1. I am addicted to things that aren't healthy for me.

_____ 2. I do things to excess even when I know better.

_____ 3. I have strong desires to escape when pressures build up.

_____ 4. I have had trouble controlling my use of alcohol, drugs, or food.

_____ 5. If I'm not very careful, I can slip *back* into bad habits easily.

Scoring: Give yourself 2 points for "yes" answers, 1 point for "in between" answers, and 0 points for "no" answers. Total your points for questions 1 through 5.

Your score = _____ (0 to 10 points)

Do You Have an Addictive Personality?

I first became aware of the connection when I was taking an evening run on the boardwalk in Belmar, New Jersey. I met a man who admitted that running was his substitute addiction. He was a recovering alcoholic, a member of AA, and an avid runner. He seemed insightful. A comment he made struck me. He said his drinking had been self-destructive, and he realized in his recovery that he was a masochist. He said running gave him a healthy outlet for his addictive personality.

I was intrigued by his observation. In discussions with other people who had trouble with substance abuse, there seemed to be a pattern of switching addictions—to find a healthy substitute for the problematic behaviors. Sometimes it was work, maybe it was meditation, some drank too much coffee, but there was usually an excessive element. The man I met on the boardwalk did marathons.

By popular acclaim, addictive disorders seem to be in vogue these days. Maybe you are a chocoholic, a workaholic, a sex addict, a drug addict, or a fitness fanatic. According to research reported in the *American Journal of Medicine*, an estimated 20% of adults seeing a physician have at one time had an alcohol problem. Dependency on prescription drugs, coupled with illegal drug usage, affects 18% to 20% of the population. And according to Patrick Carnes, a leading expert on the problem, there are 13 million Americans who are sex addicts. The redefinition of many of our behavior patterns, including smoking and codependent relationship habits, puts even more people squarely in the category of addictive personality.

Addictions are usually a way of avoiding something else—like feelings, thoughts, or perhaps reality. According to Dr. Edward Khantzian, a psychiatrist at Cambridge Hospital in Massachusetts, the prime motives for drug use are alleviation of problems and emotional pain rather than pleasure seeking. Addictions cover up the underlying need with a substitute action. So, for a while we are sated—but then the need reappears, demanding satisfaction. It is a vicious cycle that takes more than willpower to break.

"THERE GOES ANOTHER ONE OF THOSE EXERCISE ADDICTS."

According to new research reported in *Medical Self-Care*, most people who quit their bad habits do so on their own. This seems to occur in a five-stage process:

Step 1. An experience of accumulated unhappiness.

Step 2. A moment of truth—"the last straw."

Step 3. A decision to change daily patterns.

Step 4. A growing sense of control as the new patterns take hold.

Step 5. The experience of support from family and friends.

"Once an addict, always an addict." It comes as no surprise that people with addictive personalities cure themselves by forming other habits that are less damaging. Meditating twice a day, going to daily meetings, or regular exercise are popular ways of dealing with negative addictions. In fact, these have been referred to as "positive addictions." Effective treatment doesn't happen in a single shot or even on a weekly basis. Intervention must begin immediately and, at the very least, be continued on a daily schedule. As the saying goes, "One day at a time."

Exercise readily meets all six criteria for positive addictions (see "The Positive Side of Addiction," page 43), provided we keep to the rules. There is hot debate currently about whether exercise can turn into a negative addiction. In a limited study by Dr. Connie Chan at the University of Massachusetts, 75% of her exercisers were labeled as addictive. "Exercise addicts are overall competitive people hooked on a sense of control and the ability to achieve a quantifiable goal."

Dr. Chan offers four criteria to determine whether your exercise habit has turned into a negative addiction:

1. You absolutely need to exercise every day.
2. When you don't exercise, you suffer from depression, insomnia, or weight change.
3. You continue to exercise even when you have a physical injury.
4. Your whole life is planned around exercise.

These criteria should be taken seriously. I have known people who have suffered greatly from a negative exercise addiction; often the damage is irreparable by the time they recognize the problem. However, the vast majority of recreational athletes I know seem to have a positive exercise addiction. If anything, they struggle with the opposite side of this problem, that is, finding time to exercise and being regular about it. It's true you can abuse exercise just as you can abuse anything else, but I believe regular exercise is a plus for most people.

Interpreting Your Score

So what does it mean if you scored high (7 or more) on the Addictive Behaviors Quiz? The questions you answered speak for themselves. You describe yourself as getting easily hooked on things that aren't good for you, as having trouble with substances like drugs and alcohol, or as having addictive tendencies. Rather than fall prey to the downside of this analysis, you can acknowledge that this pattern will help you form a positive exercise habit.

Exercise creates its own "high"—a natural one that benefits mind and body. Researchers have identified numerous biochemical changes accompanying vigorous exercise that generate a "feel good" state. Whether it is beta-endorphins, cortisol changes, elevations in blood plasma norepinephrine, or body-temperature increases that produce the effect is not clearly known at this time. What is known, however, is that it only lasts for a matter of hours, so you have to do it all over again tomorrow. In fact, that's not so bad if you tend to be addicted to the wrong things. You need something on a daily basis to give you the boost you crave or to help smooth out those inner emotional drives.

Exercise has been called an escape, but one that can be used constructively. Psychologists talk about the benefits of time-out periods for stress reduction—and note that exercise rates high on this dimension. Exercise creates a radically different reality. It changes your mental perspective as well as releasing pent-up energy in your body. If you suffer from negative addictions, this mental and physical release will be just what you need.

Exercising to excess is the addict's enemy. Drs. Henry Abraham and Anthony Joseph from the Department of Psychiatry at Harvard Medical School offer a biochemical explanation by noting that the compulsion to induce an endorphin high may be the cause of people exercising beyond physical limits. Sociologist Barry Glassner provides a more psychological interpretation of exercise excesses: "The harder a man exercises, the more he may be trying to overcome feelings of inadequacy or helplessness." Even so, it may be the lesser of two evils. A triathlete friend made the options clear when he remarked, "If I didn't do this, I probably would develop some pretty bad habits."

The definition of excess is hard to pin down. Some people may consider a 1-mile walk excessive, but I don't think this is what the experts mean. As a recreational athlete (that is, it's not your full-time job), if you are exercising in the neighborhood of 2 or more hours a day and you fit Dr. Connie Chan's four criteria (see above), you should take a closer look at the role exercise is playing in your life and, if necessary, seek professional counseling.

The key ingredients to excess involve both time and attitude. It's unlikely that 20 minutes a day will be excessive for anybody. And attitude has to do with a sense of compulsion, a feeling that you absolutely have to exercise or your world will fall apart. When both factors are present, it's time to reassess your exercise habit.

This brings in a practical consideration. Estimates cited by Judith Elman in the July 1986 issue of *Runner's World* predict that 75% to 80% of regular runners will sooner or later sustain serious injuries. If you have an addictive personality and you can't run because of injury, you may think you're in trouble. The fallacy is believing you can't exercise if you can't run.

What you need if you score high on the Addictive Behaviors Quiz is a flexible program that incorporates different activities. Allow me a brief digression. If you review the fitness scene over the past decade, you will note the remarkable growth of multisport contests. The triathlon is only one example. Why this popularity? Many runners were suffering from overuse injuries. Sport doctors recommended rest, but when runners needed their daily fix from a 5-mile run, they ignored doctor's orders. Because patients didn't follow prescriptions, the prescriptions were changed. Doctors began recommending alternative exercises like cycling and swimming.

There are more options than swimming, running, and cycling, of course. And there are some exercise programs you can do every day without risk to your body. Examples? How about yoga or t'ai chi? An intelligent program to ensure your daily dose might include weight training coupled with aerobic exercises that use different parts of the body on different days. However, alternating between running and high-impact aerobics classes won't help. In both cases, the lower body is stressed. Swimming and running would be more complementary. Even cycling coupled with running would be less stressful than two high-impact activities back to back. You may want to take 1 or 2 days off a week. If so, consider using these days to experience the benefits of stretching. Doing long, easy stretches such as those in yoga practice can be quite pleasurable and over time may help you move away from the need to be so intense with yourself.

Maybe I can sum up advice to high scorers in the following way: The risk of getting into exercise and continuing to increase the amount until you crash has been clearly identified. To solve this problem you have to establish boundaries that are firm, clear, and nonexcessive. Once you feel secure in the regularity of your exercise habit, begin planning your workouts in a highly structured manner. Write down exactly what you are going to do each day, make sure you're not letting your mileage or time creep up, and stick to your plan. You can make your workouts reasonably hard in accordance with your fitness level, but always include ample time for cool-downs and other activities like massage to ensure an injury-free routine. Take time each day to praise yourself for being reliable and sticking to a healthy plan.

What about low scores? If your score is low (3 or less), you won't be motivated to exercise as a substitute for negative addictions. Your motivation will spring from other sources. As a low scorer, you may have to work on maintaining your connection to exercise once you start. You may be less "driven" than the high scorer, and need to continually remind yourself why you want to exercise.

The Positive Side of Addiction

Dr. William Glasser wrote *Positive Addiction* more than a decade ago. He listed six criteria for forming positive addictions:

1. The activity is noncompetitive, freely chosen, and engaged in for about 1 hour daily.
2. It is something you can do easily and without much mental effort.
3. You can do it alone—it doesn't require others' involvement.
4. It holds some physical, mental, or spiritual value for you.
5. You believe you will improve if you persist—and improvement is measured on your own scale.
6. The activity is done without self-criticism.

Weight Worry Quiz

Answer Each Question YES, NO, or IN BETWEEN
(Y = Yes   N = No   I = In between)

_____ 1. I worry about being fat or gaining weight.

_____ 2. I have problems managing my weight.

_____ 3. My self-esteem goes down when my weight goes up.

_____ 4. I would do almost anything to attain or keep a normal weight.

_____ 5. Maintaining the right weight is a high priority in my life.

Scoring: Give yourself 2 points for "yes" answers, 1 point for "in between" answers, and 0 points for "no" answers. Total your points for questions 1 through 5.

Your score = _____ (0 to 10 points)

How Heavy Is Your Weight Worry?

Fashions come and fashions go. Reed-thin models, X-ray socialites, and anorexic-looking runners are losing ground to Rubenesque beauties with soft, rounded curves that imply more than a minimum of body fat. If we can't capture the new dimensions through increased eating, hormone treatments, or plain old easy living, there's always the surgical option. According to the American Society of Plastic and Reconstructive Surgeons, 681,000 procedures were done in 1989, up 80% over 1981. One of the more popular procedures was breast augmentation, for which the rate jumped 500% in the past decade.

These indicators say more about fashion than about health and fitness. They may imply that a little of the heat is off. Couch potatoes can come out of hiding. People can quietly admit they don't exercise. And for the hard core, it's okay to drop your body-fat obsession at least 1%.

Weight problems can be roughly divided into two categories: The first we'll call obsessive and unnecessary worry, and the second we'll label reality.

Worry is reflected by statistics such as those in a study of extremely fit female long-distance runners. Researchers at the Melpomene Institute, a Minneapolis organization that researches women's health, discovered that 60% of women who were within ideal weight ranges said they were overweight. In a Canadian study, 70% of adult women expressed dissatisfaction with their weight, even though more than half were in the healthy weight range.

The *reality* issue is that close to half the adult population can be described as having overly fat bodies. More significantly, 34 million Americans are classified as clinically obese. This is cause for worry, not so much from a beauty perspective as from a health angle. Overly fat bodies are medical menaces. We become prone to a host of diseases including diabetes, heart disease, and circulatory ailments, the more weight over the recommended standard that we carry.

Whether for beauty or for health, millions of Americans follow a never-ending parade of diet fashions that promise instant "sveltehood." Dieting is often fueled by obsession about weight—but why are we so obsessed? Ironically, according to William Bennett and Joel Gurin, authors of *The Dieter's Dilemma*, the slender body that came into vogue shortly after 1910 was influenced most of all by a single factor: the liberation of women.

Experts believe that much of our weight worry is misplaced. Kim Chernin, author of *The Hungry Self*, says women struggle with their size as a substitute for struggling with their identity. According to Jane Hirschman and Carol Munter, authors of *Overcoming Overeating*, thoughts about being fat are really about something other than fat, like a feeling hidden from your awareness. Hirschman and Munter believe these "fat thoughts" are never about being fat. When someone feels fat, what's really going on is an unidentified anxiety arising from some want, need, feeling, or thought that seems forbidden or beyond reach.

Clinical psychologist Erica Wise agrees. Writing in *Shape* magazine, Dr. Wise notes that "when you're feeling fat, there's also another aspect of your life that isn't going well—some problem that you may be ignoring." The idea is that weight worry is a convenient scapegoat. When you listen to your mind complaining about your weight, you get distracted from what is really bothering you. Wise suggests that "realistic self-acceptance will help you get rid of your fat feelings. What you need to do is develop an increased appreciation of yourself."

"ALL THIS READING ABOUT EXERCISE IS HELPING ME KEEP MY WEIGHT DOWN!"

It may not be the same for men. In a study of college freshmen, 85% of the women and only 45% of the men wanted to lose weight. More poignantly, 40% of the men wanted to gain weight—something only an insignificant percentage of the women wanted to do. Another gender difference of note was that most of the women tried to control their weight through dieting, whereas the men exercised.

Unfortunately, most diets are misguided. Strict dieting without exercise typically results in the loss of more muscle than fat. When we starve ourselves, the body goes into emergency operation, reacting as if it were trying to survive a 10-year famine. More energy is stored in fat cells than in muscle, so in the wisdom of the body, muscle is judged more expendable. The end result is a body that is lighter but remains overly fat. Not only is this an unhealthy state, but it's not particularly attractive.

The American College of Sports Medicine recommends a combination of moderate dieting plus exercise as the most effective and medically sound means of losing weight. The exercise component consists of a minimum of three aerobic exercise sessions per week, with each session lasting 20 to 30 minutes. If there is a choice to be made between dieting and exercising, exercising should be the winner. Dr. Grant Gwinup, an endocrinologist at the University of California-Irvine, found that walking or cycling vigorously at least 30 minutes a day results in significant weight loss *even without dieting*.

Interpreting Your Score

If you score high (7 or more) on the Weight Worry Quiz, you are likely to show high concern over fluctuations on the bathroom scale. Incidentally, this doesn't necessarily mean you are overweight, rather that you worry about your weight. If you are overweight and want to do something about it, a general rule is to check with your doctor first and then begin a well-advised program of dieting plus exercise.

Are some exercises better than others? Indeed. Many overweight people start an exercise program with misinformation. I often find them in the weight room or on high-tech body-building machines. Wrong! If you need to lose weight, why do exercises to make you look like Mr. or Ms. Universe? It's not going to work—at least, not for a year or so—and you are likely to get discouraged long before that. Weight training strengthens your muscles but may be a slow way to lose fat. You would do better with an aerobic workout.

I know, your first objection is that you weigh too much to run. Your second objection is you are embarrassed to go to an aerobics class. Okay, objections understood. What about walking? Or cycling? Or low-impact aerobics in front of your TV?

What about swimming? Well, you may hedge on swimming because you read something about how swimming doesn't help much with weight loss. It's true there is a debate about whether swimming is as good as other aerobic workouts for achieving weight loss. But one thing is certain. Swimming won't be of much benefit to weight loss if you spend most of your pool time floating rather than racing back and forth. Rick Sharpe, the director of the exercise physiology lab at Iowa State University, identifies two ineffective types of swimmers: floaters and thrashers. Swimming with improper stroke, kick, or body movement will prevent you from getting maximum aerobic benefit and, therefore, limit weight loss. The conclusion? The jury is out on whether swimming is as effective for weight loss as other aerobic exercise, but it is far better than being sedentary. If you are considerably overweight, you will want to avoid high-impact activities until you shed some of the excess weight. (That extra weight puts you at greater risk of injury.) Consider swimming as part of your program. As a no-impact activity, it can be relaxing as well as invigorating. But if your swimming style needs improvement, find a coach or take lessons. The long-term benefits are well worth an initial investment.

Another controversy surrounds the question of whether low- to moderate-intensity exercise is better than high-intensity exercise for burning fat. This is based on some physiological considerations about how the body stores energy and then uses it when we exercise. Most experts subscribe to the belief that weight loss will vary in proportion to two factors: how long and how hard you exercise. This means that if you exercise at low to moderate intensity (for example, taking brisk walks), you will have to continue longer than if you exercise at high intensity (for example, running) to burn up the same number of calories. Another way of saying this is that 30 minutes doesn't necessarily equal 30 minutes—what matters is how hard you exercise during those 30 minutes.

The bottom line is there are no safe shortcuts. If you want to lose weight, increasing the intensity of your workouts so you can burn more calories is likely to result in injury, especially if you are not in shape. Acknowledge what your goals are, and allow the time necessary to achieve them. After all, long walks can be quite enjoyable.

You can always find examples that make weight loss look easy. Remar Sutton's book, *Body Worry*, provides an entertaining account of how he went from being a flabby 201 pounds to being a 163-pound muscular hulk in 1 year. If you read carefully, you will note that Mr. Sutton spent nearly $100,000 on his weight-loss program. Fortunately, he recouped some of it through royalties on his entertaining story. Not all of us can take a year off, move to a Caribbean island, and hire a bunch of personal trainers. So, plan carefully. Set modest goals. And stick with it. If you commit yourself to losing weight through exercise, you will do it—in time.

There's another side to weight worry. According to Dr. Margot Weinshel, therapist and coauthor of *Surviving an Eating Disorder*, the new malady of the '90s is exercise bulimia. Weight is the governing factor in the lives of exercise bulimics, and excessive exercise is the mechanism of control instead of purging. Dr. Rebecca Prussin, a psychiatrist at Mt. Sinai Medical Center in New York, says that "vigorous exercise to prevent weight gain is one of the diagnostic criteria for bulimics. Weight gain is the one fear in their lives they can control." If you are considerably underweight, obsessed about getting fat, and addicted to long, intense workouts, there is a value judgment you have to make. From a medical perspective, you may be running out of time—a daily diet of 2 to 3 hours of high-impact aerobics takes its toll on your body. If you score high on the Weight Worry Quiz and you are significantly below the standard for your height, you may want to delve deeper into this matter—for instance, by asking yourself, "What is really fueling my weight worry?" You might consider changing your program if you are hooked on high-impact activities. Maybe a little body shaping or weight work, or even something fun like a team sport? It could also be of value to talk your program over with a professional counselor who is familiar with the exercise world. You may need support while you are making adjustments in your routine.

If your score is low (3 or less), there is a fundamental question you should answer before dismissing this motive and moving on to other potential motivators: From a medical perspective, do you maintain a healthy weight? If you're not sure, check with your doctor. If the answer is yes, there's little reason to have weight worry become a pivotal factor in designing your exercise plan. If your answer is no, make a note to come back to this quiz later on. You may find in an upcoming quiz that your self-esteem is on the low side so that worrying about weight hasn't even surfaced in your life's priorities. The point to bear in mind is, if your score is low and your weight deviates from healthy standards, why aren't you concerned? What else is consuming your attention? You are likely to find out in the remaining quizzes, so—for now—put this one aside with a promise to revisit it later on.

At work, Nancy was a star, at home she was a supermom, and in her leisure time she was a great athlete. Seven days a week, Nancy ran 5 to 6 miles before her kids got up for breakfast. She slipped in a noontime aerobics or circuit-training class during the week and a "SuperFit" class on the weekend. She was 5-foot-5 and weighed 110 pounds. Underneath it all, she was utterly obsessed about getting fat. In private, she admitted to having been bulimic as a teenager, but she felt that was behind her—until she was diagnosed as having stress fractures and had to stop *cold*. She was lucky enough to find a good therapist who helped her through the withdrawal and depression from not running, and who directed her toward a less abusive exercise program. It took over a year before she could let go of her weight worry and begin enjoying life—including a synchronized swimming class.

--------------------------- **Health Worry Quiz** ---------------------------

Answer Each Question YES, NO, or IN BETWEEN
(Y = Yes   N = No   I = In between)

_____ 1. I worry about getting sick and losing my health.

_____ 2. I fear I might die at a young age due to diseases like cancer and heart ailments.

_____ 3. My family's health history makes me worry about my own health.

_____ 4. I am extremely aware of the nutritional benefits and liabilities of all the foods I eat.

_____ 5. I usually buy books and magazines on topics of health care and disease prevention.

Scoring: Give yourself 2 points for "yes" answers, 1 point for "in between" answers, and 0 points for "no" answers. Total your points for questions 1 through 5.

Your score = _____ (0 to 10 points)

Your Health—How Worried Are You?

You don't have to live in California to want to live a long and vigorous life. Californians may be more likely to add "beautiful" to the equation as they lather themselves in sunscreen, down bottles of mineral water, and salivate over 100% organically grown salads. But what's wrong with that?

As we move into the 21st century, the prospect of a long and healthy life dangles in front of us like the proverbial carrot. Dr. Ken Dychtwald, author of *Age Wave* and guru to the gathering hordes of senior citizens, tells us how much our world will change in future decades as the locus of power shifts to golden-agers who will possess most of the wealth, own most of the property, and in numbers constitute the largest political block in Western society.

As some people contemplate life at 90, others worry they will never make it to 60. Part of their worry may be well founded. Popular magazines carry quizzes that help predict your longevity based on factors like heredity, health history, diet, and lifestyle. We have some control over all but heredity—theoretically speaking, of course. Try telling a smoker to quit because he is jeopardizing his health, and you know how intractible our habits can be.

Some people mask their fears of mortality beneath a "devil may care" attitude. We can be incredibly shortsighted when it comes to guarding our health. And it's not always the big things that matter, but rather our responses to questions like these:

Do you always wear a seatbelt when in a car?

Do you floss your teeth daily?

Do you wear sunscreen when you go outside?

Do you exercise regularly?

It takes special effort to stay healthy, and many people operate under mistaken notions such as a belief that health is a given or that diseases are like lotteries, a matter of luck. They ignore warning signs of illness, or they fail to take simple health precautions. Lung cancer is a horror, but few smokers preview the future by spending time with cancer patients. It comes as no surprise, therefore, that 94% of the health dollars in the United States go to curative medicine and only about 3% to prevention.

Fortunately, there is another side—about people who are concerned with their health and who do whatever is in their power to remain healthy. This is the side that connects with the exercise habit.

A few years back, Dr. Ralph Paffenbarger described the results of a longitudinal study of Harvard graduates in the *New England Journal of Medicine*. He found that the more these graduates exercised in their adult years, the greater was their life expectancy. His findings were summarized in a formula that projected 2 extra hours of lifetime for every hour a person exercised.

Since this initial report, Dr. Paffenbarger has uncovered additional evidence indicating that people who exercise regularly have a lower incidence of illnesses like cancer and coronary heart disease. Other investigators have reached similar conclusions, and some have added to the list of diseases that may be retarded or prevented by exercise. Diabetes, osteoporosis, arthritis, cancer, and hypertension are just a few of the health problems thought to be prevented by programs of regular exercise. As one concrete demonstration of the buffering powers of exercise, Dr. Raymond Flannery, assistant professor of psychology at Harvard Medical School, found that 80% of students who were rarely sick engaged in regular aerobic exercise, compared to only 20% of students who had high rates of illness.

Interpreting Your Score

Your score on the Health Worry Quiz reflects your concern about health issues. Having a high score (7 or more) doesn't mean you are in poor health; rather, it may mean that you want to do whatever you can to remain healthy. It may be that your family has a history of cancer or heart disease, and you are tuned in to preventive health practices. Very high scores translate into high concern and lots of worry.

If you score high, chances are you are involved in some form of exercise—and that your goal is health. You may already know that exercise strengthens your immune system and makes you more resilient to disease. According to Owen Anderson, moderate exercise programs boost immunity by increasing the production of adrenaline, a hormone that mobilizes disease-vanquishing white blood cells. Physical activity also promotes the release of the hormone cortisol, which temporarily stimulates white cells so they are more available to fight infection.

As a high scorer, you might take your daily dose of exercise as a medical prescription and religiously adhere to the proper dosage. You know how much exercise is required for health maintenance and are not likely to jeopardize your health by doing too much or too little. The American College of Sports Medicine's recommendations for exercise may be just where you target your exercise level.

It's also possible that you score high and avoid exercise for fear it might be injurious to your health. If this is the case, you need a second opinion. For instance, people who have concerns about the occurrence or recurrence of coronary heart disease may mistakenly believe they should not exercise. Granted it's not a good idea to train for a marathon, but there are numerous exercise forms that can be extremely beneficial. Many health clubs have "coronary aftercare" exercise programs designed for people who are recovering from heart disease. Having a triple bypass operation doesn't mean no exercise. You just need to get sound advice and ongoing coaching. Look for a good aftercare program that is supervised and medically monitored.

Special exercise programs have also been developed for individuals suffering from conditions like diabetes and arthritis. Having one of these conditions won't prevent you from exercising—it just means you have to recognize what will work best for you. Usually a slow progression from one activity level to the next is advised, as is the avoidance of exercises, such as high-impact aerobics, that may aggravate such conditions as arthritis.

The guiding principle for health-conscious people is moderation. In this respect, you will be heartened by Dr. Bryant Stamford's new book, *Fitness Without Exercise*, which advocates the redefinition of household chores and fun activities as exercise. He says, "If we haven't been able to convince people to jog with 20 years of propaganda, it's time for a new approach." Going along with Stamford's thesis, a recent article in the November 1989 issue of the *Journal of the American Medical Association* found that even if you exercise as little as a 20-minute walk two or three times a week, you can reduce your risk of early death from cancer and heart disease by half.

If health is your strongest motivation, you need to guard against fixating on the physiological aspects of your exercise program. Exercising solely out of fear of disease or death can be grim and joyless. Limiting yourself to activities like walking on a treadmill that enable you to keep your heart rate under close observation may prevent you from obtaining other health-related benefits of exercise. Sure, you can distract yourself from the discomfort of cycling on a stationary bicycle by watching the news, but there are other things you can do that are more directly pleasurable. Depending on your age and physical condition, there are activities like yoga and swimming that make you feel good while exercising. In fact, swimming rates as one of the best life-extending, life-enhancing, lifelong workout programs around. It is seen as a "low-impact, whole-body aerobic exercise, a terrific torso toner, even a meditative mind relaxer," according to Jennifer Drawbridge, reporting in *Longevity* magazine.

There are various forms of dance, ranging from modern to social dance, that may add new zest to your life. If team sports put you at risk, try exercising with a friend, because social contact is critically important to health. In brief, consider ways of varying your routine or adding the element of fun. As Norman Cousins told us in his autobiography, *Anatomy of an Illness*, joy and laughter can be pretty good medicine.

As a low scorer (3 or less), make sure you aren't avoiding health concerns before looking elsewhere for your exercise motivation. Were you being realistic about your health risks and lifestyle (for example, smoking and drinking habits) when you completed this quiz? If not, recognize your cavalier attitude toward health may mask more fundamental questions about your self-worth. Should you detect an inconsistency between your real health risks and your breezy attitudes toward your health, be on the watch for other signs of a poor self concept in the remaining quizzes.

The Jim Fixx story is one that keeps coming up when people want to justify sedentary lifestyles. Jim Fixx was the running guru who died at age 49 from heart disease, even though he kept up a daily regimen of running 5 to 10 miles. The counterargument is that Fixx, who suffered from congenital heart disease, probably would have died at an even younger age if it hadn't been for his passion for running. Neither side can ever prove its point, but medical evidence weighs heavily on the side of exercising as a preventive measure for a host of illnesses, including heart disease. If you suffer from coronary heart disease or some other illness, how much exercise is good for you is a matter of medical opinion. Even so, it's unlikely that any doctor will recommend permanent bed rest! This brings us back to the definition of exercise. It doesn't mean running marathons, nor is it the annual fishing trip. It is something regular and active—and with that minimal definition, the options are unlimited.

Quest for Youth Quiz

Answer Each Question YES, NO, or IN BETWEEN
(Y = Yes   N = No   I = In between)

_____ 1. I worry about losing my vitality as I grow older.

_____ 2. I devote time and energy to doing things to stay young.

_____ 3. The thought of growing old frightens me.

_____ 4. I am aware of all the gradual signs of aging in my physical and mental functioning.

_____ 5. Keeping up a youthful lifestyle is important to me.

Scoring: Give yourself 2 points for "yes" answers, 1 point for "in between" answers, and 0 points for "no" answers. Total your points for questions 1 through 5.

Your score = _____ (0 to 10 points)

Are You an Age-a-Phobic?

Exercise physiologists have charts that project our decline. For each year over 30, we lose about 1% of our muscle mass per year. Our $\dot{V}O_2$max, the greatest amount of oxygen one can consume when working, declines such that at age 50 we have about 70% of what we had at age 20. We know where the gains are—where we least want them, in percentages of body fat and overall weight. We are told that youthfulness is largely a state of mind, but it is extremely hard to reconcile an aging ego with these physical facts of life. The problem is not just personal but societal. By the year 2025, Americans over 65 are expected to outnumber teenagers by more than 2 to 1, and the median age of Americans will surpass the critical age-40 mark.

The other day I was watching some of my colleagues at a faculty meeting. The average age in the group was somewhere in the mid-40s (young!), but I was struck by the stiff, ponderous movements of most of the professors. It was a long meeting, about 3 hours with no break, and when it was over, I observed the slow, shuffling exits of the brain-weary participants. They looked like they belonged in a geriatric ward. Some of these people exercised, most did not. Maybe they thought they were too old or too busy for such activity.

Another memory comes to mind. It is of an Aikido workshop where most participants were also in their mid-40s. Aikido is a Japanese form of the martial arts that involves tumbling, twists, flips, and turns, along with other techniques of evasion. You have to keep limber and flexible in Aikido. When you fall, you want to hit the ground with the looseness of a Raggedy Ann doll and the responsiveness of a tiger. Need I say that these people didn't shuffle?

Curiously, the difference may not be entirely between exercise and no exercise, but in many cases it results from the kind of exercise you do. Years ago when I studied dance, I had a teacher who talked about the importance of spinal flexibility for a youthful body. She could ripple her spine like a serpent, moving her vertebrae one at a time. It was fascinating—and so was she. At the tender age of 50, she had more energy than anyone I knew. She simply sparkled.

This message about keeping your spine flexible for that youthful feeling is a popular one. In my encounters with such disciplines as modern dance, martial arts, yoga, as well as some of the healing arts like Feldenkreis and Alexander technique, the same message is repeated, not to mention demonstrated in the lives of people who practice these movement forms.

There are two points I want to bring out. First, our bodies change significantly over the decades, but the effects of aging have much to do with how we live. Research consistently shows that people who exercise regularly feel more energetic. Professor Robert Rikli of California State University in Fullerton tested women whose average age was 70 and who had been exercising three times per week for 15 years or longer. He found their reaction times to be almost identical to those of inactive college-age women. According to Dr. Willibald Nagler of Cornell University Medical College, how fast or slow our bodies age isn't just a matter of genes. A lot depends on how much or how little we use our bodies throughout life. By staying active, Dr. Nagler believes you can hold off or even prevent many of the so-called normal effects of aging by as much as 70%. The bottom line seems to be "Use it or lose it!"

The American Academy of Physical Education summarized some of the benefits of exercise in a 1989 paper on "Physical Activity and Aging." Weight loss, lowered risk of cardiovascular disease, prevention of osteoporosis, and increased muscle mass represent a few of the reliable rewards of regular exercise. According to exercise scientists Craig Cisar and Len Kravitz, writing in the January 1991 issue of Idea Today, "Physical activity may be the closest thing we have to that long-sought-after Fountain of Youth!"

A second point is that although most health-conscious people believe in the positive effects of exercise for slowing the aging process, there is good reason to believe that some exercise programs *or* some ways of doing exercise are better than others.

Interpreting Your Score

Before interpreting your score, let's be clear about what we are discussing. This exercise motive won't give you something as easy as a drink from the fountain of youth, but it will show you how to increase your chances of aging gracefully, of looking and feeling as good as you can for as long as you can. Addressing this motive through exercise won't help you erase wrinkles, or work quickly like a hormone injection that reverses signs of aging. It isn't about cosmetic changes—it concerns something deeper about the way you want to live and feel.

The motive analyzed in the Quest for Youth Quiz measures your concern about feeling youthful and maintaining an energetic lifestyle. Low scores (3 or less) suggest you may accept aging as a natural process and are not particularly motivated to take extra measures to retard the aging process. On the other hand, if you score high on this quiz (7 or more), you want to stave off signs of aging. You want to be active and keep your body young. If you score high, you have a solid incentive to get into shape—and stay that way. The question is, what's the best program for you?

Recognize that your motivation has a lot to do with an internal feeling you have about your body as well as its external appearance. If you look good on the outside, but feel terrible inside, you won't be happy. Your body needs different kinds of exercise at different ages. A 16-year-old may be able to run 5 miles without warming up or cooling down, and suffer few side effects. It's a different story if you are 50.

If you trace the movements of a child throughout the day and contrast them with those of an adult in a sedentary job, you notice remarkable discrepancies in the range and types of movements each makes. What this tells us is that we have to do a lot of rehabilitative work on a daily basis as we get older just to prevent deterioration of some of our muscle groups. Exercise programs that are very specific, that work limited areas of the body, like the legs, require supplemental activities. Runners, for instance, are advised to do weight training for the upper body to keep the muscles toned, and to include a complete stretching program for flexibility. It is perhaps no coincidence that cross-training is one of the hottest fitness trends of the 1990s.

What you must recognize in this emphasis on youthfulness is that you must keep the whole body tuned. It isn't enough to have a good cardiovascular workout. Your program needs to be complete and should include work on flexibility. Oftentimes what makes you look and feel old is the way your body moves. If your joints are stiff, if your motions are tight, if your body moves like a concrete block rather than with the suppleness of a child, you look old—you feel old.

Maybe your program needs to incorporate massage or therapeutic body work. By consulting an expert who can tell you where you are tight or what muscles need toning, you can begin to put together an exercise program that will keep your movements fluid and your energy flowing.

The payoffs are undeniable. According to Dr. Roy Shephard, director of the School of Physical and Health Education at the University of Toronto, "A sedentary person who goes into training can produce a response that may be the equivalent of a 10 year or even a 20 year rejuvenation." Says Shephard, "I don't think there's any form of medication that can match that."

Murray is 55 years old and has been running for 30 years. Until recently, running was his only activity. He averages over 50 miles a week, which isn't particularly easy when winter rolls around. His body is slim and muscular, but he has little flexibility in his movements. His motions are tight and jerky. He looks weathered and a bit older than his years, but Murray isn't particularly worried about how he looks. What he likes about running is that it *gives him energy*. He feels younger than his years, and his work habits prove it. The junior staff in his law firm have a hard time keeping up with him. One day recently, he slowed down long enough to be reflective, and commented to a trainer at his club, "Lately I've been feeling old and stiff—I never used to feel this way." The trainer, who knew Murray's routine, suggested some yoga classes. Murray answered with a laugh, "Who me? You've got to be kidding!" The trainer responded, "What's the alternative?"

Murray's story provides a good example of how exercise helps, but also of how it could be even better. Although Murray doesn't appear very youthful, it would be difficult to prove this is simply the result of running. There are a few additional facts you have to consider. They concern the *way* Murray exercises. Murray is the architect of his body. In the weight room, you can see him speeding through the machines like the "roadrunner" he is. He's fast, his movements are spastic, and he never goes through the full range of movement. Worst of all, he doesn't believe in stretching. The lack of flexibility Murray manifests in his movements is a result of his approach to exercise. Murray isn't alone—in fact, he may be in the majority.

Reviewing Your Body Motives

You have analyzed six body motives and seen how they can reinforce your efforts to develop or maintain the exercise habit. Be aware of which scores are high and which are low. Keep in mind what you need to fuel your motivation, especially how you may have to tailor your program to suit your motivations.

Completing Your Profile

A graph is provided in Figure 3.1 so you can create a visual overview of your scores. Write your six body motive scores in the spaces provided on the graph. On the left side of the graph, you will find a scale ranging from 0 to 10. Start with your score on the Vanity Quiz. Draw a line corresponding to your score (0 to 10) across the top of the Vanity column. Then shade in the area in the column beneath the line. Do the same for the other motives.

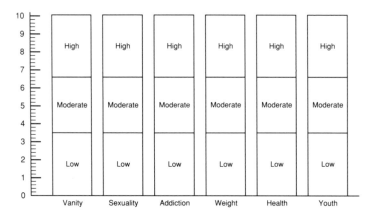

Figure 3.1   In the graph above, each column represents one of the six body motives. For each, draw a line corresponding to your score across the column, then shade in the area below your line.

The Body Motives Profile you have just created will help you compare your six scores. You can determine which is your highest and lowest. If your body motives are uniformly high, it will call your attention to the potency of these motives for supporting an exercise habit. Conversely, if they are uniformly low, it tells you to look to other motives to reinforce an exercise program.

Take a few minutes to consider what this graph says about you. Question yourself about any reactions to this profile. Does it make sense to you? Does it accurately portray who you are? Do you feel good about it? Make notes on your reactions so you have a record of things you might want to emphasize or change as you go about designing an exercise program in later chapters.

We will now leave the body motives for the moment and turn to an analysis of your psychological and social motives. When we are done creating these profiles, we will come back to compare all three sets of motives to determine their relative strengths as motivations for the exercise habit.

CHAPTER 4

YOUR PSYCHOLOGICAL MOTIVES AND HOW TO USE THEM

"I came for my body and stayed for my mind."
ANONYMOUS

Do you

- suffer from a poor self-image?
- seek a new challenge for your ego?
- ride the roller coaster of emotional highs and lows?
- need a way to manage your stress?
- lack a sense of meaning in your life?
- want an outlet for your playful spirit?

If you answered "yes" to *any* of these questions, keep reading. The psychological motives described in this chapter may be keys to your personal fulfillment through exercise.

What Are Your Psychological Motives?

How does exercise play into your psychological motives? The answer comes from appreciating some basic truths about yourself, like the fact that each of us has a need to feel good about ourselves. We call this self-esteem. What this chapter will illustrate is how self-esteem can be developed through exercise. We also have a need to feel challenged. We set valued goals so that we can feel the satisfaction of achieving them. Exercise can help with that, too.

Integral to a sense of well-being is our ability to master emotions and manage stress. Emotions such as anxiety and depression are part of that scenario. Weighed down by life concerns, we may succumb to feelings of depression or we worry ourselves sick. When pressure builds up we have to find ways of releasing the steam—or suffer the consequences. Exercise is the antidote to stress and emotional disease for millions of people. Why not for you?

At a deeper level, psychologists have written about our need for meaning in life. This may sound a bit mystical—it is. A parent may find meaning in raising children, a monk may find significance in prayer. It differs for each of us, and unfortunately one of the major ailments of our time is that many people are lost souls, lacking an orienting purpose in life. We will see how exercise addresses this problem.

Our last psychological motive is most special. Ironically, by the time we remember its value, we may have squelched its vitality so thoroughly that it is like raising the dead to bring it back into our lives. It is the motive of play—a spirit of laughter and childlike abandon. Playfulness means letting go, loosening the bonds on our ego—a total release into being. It is a freedom from self-consciousness, from the *shoulds* and *have-tos*, and an awakening of the sprite that lives in each of us. Needless to say, this is a unique gift that exercise offers our weary adult psyches.

How do you rate on these motives, and, more critically, what do you need to satisfy them?

Self-Esteem Quiz

Answer Each Question YES, NO, or IN BETWEEN
(Y = Yes   N = No   I = In between)

_____ 1. When I compare myself to others, I get the feeling they are somehow better than me.

_____ 2. I get upset with myself whenever I make mistakes.

_____ 3. I have a hard time accepting myself as I am.

_____ 4. If I could be anyone in the world, I would choose to be someone other than myself.

_____ 5. I don't seem to say or do very much that is worthwhile.

Scoring: Give yourself 2 points for "yes" answers, 1 point for "in between" answers, and 0 points for "no" answers. Total your points for questions 1 through 5.

Your score = _____ (0 to 10 points)

Self-Esteem—How Do You Rate?

What is self-esteem? You might say it's whether you have positive or negative feelings about yourself. Of course, most people would say they have both positive and negative feelings about themselves. So, then, it's something like the average of all our self-attitudes. Depending on whether the pluses outweigh the minuses, our self-esteem ends up as either positive, negative, or somewhere in between.

Interest in self-esteem has mushroomed in the past quarter-century. Between 1979 and 1985 alone, one researcher indexed 1,416 articles, 50 manuscripts, and 30 psychological tests of self-esteem. As a society, we have become obsessed by self-analysis. This acute interest in the self parallels a growing fragmentation of society. People are isolated not only through the deterioration of family structures and community groups, but also by a persistent push for introspection and self-awareness.

A potential result of this emphasis on the self has been identified by Dr. Martin Seligman, University of Pennsylvania professor of psychology and noted author of an incisive study of depression, *Learned Helplessness*. Citing an alarming statistic about the tenfold increase in emotional depression within the yuppie generation when compared to their elders, Dr. Seligman explains: "Something about our society has made us increasingly vulnerable to depression—not just the blues but serious clinical problems." According to Seligman, the root cause can be traced to the changing theories of human behavior. Starting in the 1960s, the site of action shifted from outside the self to within the self. Whatever happens in your life is up to you. You're in charge. You press the buttons that make things happen. We have exalted the individual to impossible levels. The heat is on. We have to be aware—and if the product of our awareness is a sense of inadequacy, we alone are responsible. It's our *fault*.

Dr. Seligman's point is that when people who feel inadequate are now told that the responsibility for their bad feelings is all their own and that it is entirely up to them to make themselves feel better, they are not likely to jump to the task with great optimism. More likely, they will feel overwhelmed and sink into depression.

A poor self-concept is dangerous. It undermines us through self-sabotage and each time we fail, it grows like cancer. A great many personal and societal problems result from the fact that people don't have enough self-esteem and try to compensate through actions that are injurious to self and others. Suicide is an extreme way of taking care of bad feelings about oneself, but failing in school, extramarital affairs, poor health habits, and shoddy work behaviors can also be manifestations of negative self-attitudes.

Self-esteem isn't always constant. Life events and our ways of coping can send our egos on perilous journeys from omnipotence to despair. We may rebound for the next encounter, but too many wounds to our egos can put us at risk. A good way to take control of a roller-coastering ego is to understand where self-esteem comes from—and how we can strengthen it.

Self-esteem derives from three sources: what we do, how well we do it, and feelings about our bodies. What we do translates into the roles we play in the world. It's the answer to the question "Who am I?"—wife, mother, daughter, attorney, friend, and tennis player! Having multiple roles in the world increases the chances that we will at least have good feelings about some of the parts we play in life.

The second source of self-esteem comes from our skills and abilities—in a sense, how well we play our roles. The more we learn about what we do and the greater our efforts to be consistent and skillful in our roles, the more self-satisfaction we derive. It may be expressed as a pride in craftwork or as an acknowledgment of having done something difficult.

Finally, our bodies and how we feel about them enter the picture. In this body-conscious society, body esteem forms a major slice of overall self-esteem. In fact, a June 1990 *Self* magazine survey report showed that 41% of survey respondents connected their self-esteem directly to their body image.

Vicki's career was like a day-old glass of Perrier. No sparkle, no pizzaz—just flat. Her ego felt the same. Even so, Vicki was a workaholic. She couldn't uncouple from the demands of work. Maybe it was her doctor's warning about her rising blood pressure or the vacuum she experienced when her workday ended. Whatever the cause, she took up running as a hobby. At first, it was once or twice a week. By summer she had joined a running club, and by fall she completed a 20K race sponsored by the "Y." She quit smoking, cut back on work, and began feeling better about herself. It seemed miraculous. Though she sensed that her running had something to do with it, she couldn't quite grasp how something as simple as exercise could make such a big difference.

There are solid reasons why exercise will help build self-esteem—and they are not limited to making you feel better about your body. Consider Vicki and her "miraculous" transformation. At age 35, Vicki was suffering from low self-esteem but had only minor complaints about her body. Her muscles were getting a bit flabby, but she was lucky—she had always been thin and wiry, and as the years had passed, her body had shown only minimal signs of aging. So apparently the erosion of her self-esteem wasn't due to body changes. What was its cause, then? Vicki's identity was wrapped in a career that had become stale for her. By adding exercise to her life, Vicki gave herself a new identity—she became a runner. Not only was this an addition to her life roles, but she also demonstrated real skill. She competed in a half marathon—and finished with a respectable time! Exercise boosted all three sources of Vicki's self-esteem: Her body felt better, and even though she didn't have too many complaints about it before, she enjoyed seeing the muscular development in her calves and thighs. Her self-definition grew from that of a unidimensional drone to that of a more expanded person who had interests outside of work. And her success in running was the icing on the cake.

Gordon Ainsleigh, the top runner in the 1974 Western States Endurance Race, a 100-mile gauntlet, captured the exercise effect on self-esteem: "[Running] gives me a chance to face my worst enemy, which is myself, and to meet my best friend, which is also myself. You face your enemy and deal with him as best you can, and you face your best friend and embrace him."

Interpreting Your Score

The more "yes" answers you had to the Self-Esteem Quiz, the less you accept yourself—and the less likely it is that you do things to keep yourself psychologically and physically tuned-up.

Will exercise help you? If you rated 7 or more on the Self-Esteem Quiz (high scores mean low self-esteem), participation in a regular exercise program should help. Research consistently reports that athletes have higher self-esteem than nonathletes. Even though you will find some very self-satisfied folks who don't exercise in the narrow sense of the term (aerobics, running, weights, etc.), chances are that these high-self-esteem-ers lead very active lifestyles.

If your self-esteem is low and you don't exercise, what should you do? According to Dorothy Harris, professor of exercise and sports science at Penn State University, an important step is acknowledging that "exercise is a selfish venture, *in the most positive sense.*" Harris believes we need to shift to "a personal way of evaluating the value and benefits of fitness. You only do it for yourself." The key is accepting that it's okay to do something good for yourself—that you deserve it.

Next, you want to find an activity you like and one you will stay with. You don't need another failure experience. Part III of *The Exercise Habit* provides sound advice on what to do to stay on track.

What if you exercise and your self-esteem is low? That's possible—and quitting is not the answer. It's unlikely you will feel better about yourself if you switch to a sedentary lifestyle. There are some questions that may help identify the problem.

Are you involved in an unrewarding, no-fun activity? Consider how you feel while you are working out. Do you like how you feel? Do you enjoy the body sensations exercise gives you? Do you like the environment where you train or the people with whom you exercise? If you exercise alone, would you like it more if you had a partner?

Are your exercise goals reasonable? It may be that your goals are too high or that you compare yourself to others who are out of your league. Did you expect to have lost a certain amount of weight by now or to have achieved a higher level of performance? Did you think you should be as flexible and coordinated as the aerobics instructor by this time? What were your goals, and was there a self-defeating element to the way you set them? Here's an example of an underlying statement that accompanies unrealistic goals: "I'll never achieve these goals, and that will prove once again how worthless I am and that I will never get anything I want in life!" Give yourself a break. You can do remarkable things—but it takes time. Be persistent, and above all, be patient with yourself. Pat yourself on the back for trying.

Is there something else you are doing that is dragging your self-esteem down? Maybe your exercise program is keeping you from crashing altogether. Other lifestyle considerations may be contributing to your decline. If you don't already know what these factors are, you might get some useful information in the upcoming discussions of exercise motives. So keep reading.

How does this discussion relate to low scores (3 or less)? If your score is low, the interpretation is that your self-esteem is in fine shape. You seem to like and accept yourself, and tolerate those times when you are less than perfect. In all likelihood, physical activity is part of your life, perhaps not in a formal way, but as a pattern of keeping active and on the go. If you're not involved in a regular exercise program, ask yourself what you would need to change to make exercise part of life. It's a good insurance policy.

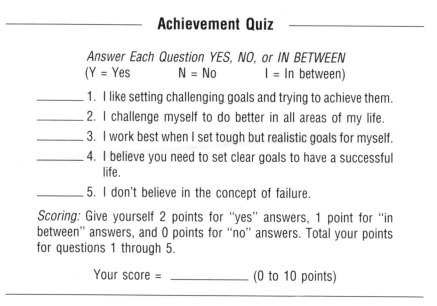

Achievement Quiz

Answer Each Question YES, NO, or IN BETWEEN
(Y = Yes   N = No   I = In between)

_____ 1. I like setting challenging goals and trying to achieve them.

_____ 2. I challenge myself to do better in all areas of my life.

_____ 3. I work best when I set tough but realistic goals for myself.

_____ 4. I believe you need to set clear goals to have a successful life.

_____ 5. I don't believe in the concept of failure.

Scoring: Give yourself 2 points for "yes" answers, 1 point for "in between" answers, and 0 points for "no" answers. Total your points for questions 1 through 5.

Your score = _____ (0 to 10 points)

Your Need to Achieve

Some people seem driven. They operate with an internalized ringmaster who keeps asking them to jump higher and strive for what others might consider impossible. The fact is, all of us have at one point or another set our sights high and started after something we dreamed about. If we got what we were after, it encouraged us enough to set another goal. Eventually this notion of goal setting became habitual.

Or perhaps we didn't get the brass ring on the carousel—and gave up. We developed a fear of failure that prevented us from setting our sights much beyond our immediate reach.

Society wants us to have a strong achievement motive. We are taught that achieving is good, that trying hard builds character, and that the absence of a will to succeed is a guarantee of mediocrity. Experts tell us how to build this achievement motive. There are courses in goal setting, and large corporations devote millions of dollars and countless hours each year to programs like "Management by Objectives" that are thoroughly grounded in the achievement motive.

The downside is that many societal structures may be hypocritical, in that they wave the flag of achievement motivation yet deny us the means to satisfy the need. Relatively few jobs make achievement experiences part of the daily routine. Consider the assembly line, as a prime example. Not only is the individual's behavior governed by the pacing of a machine, but in most cases the worker knows that her job will eventually be performed faster and more accurately by another machine. How can she feel a sense of accomplishment in this environment?

Outside the work world, achievement opportunities may be equally remote or obscured by uncertain results. Take the example of parenting. Most parents live in confusion about the effectiveness of their efforts. "Did I do the right thing?" "Will she grow up well-adjusted?" "Do I push harder or back off completely?"

So the big picture is one of parents plagued with doubts about their actions, workers caught in lockstep bureaucracies or mind-numbing automation—and where success is identifiable in our world, we hear complaints that it's who you know that really counts. So, where can we satisfy the need to achieve?

In the context of this book, the answer may seem obvious. If you are a disbeliever, go to your local newsstand and browse through copies of *Runner's World, Triathlete,* or *Muscle and Fitness.* Granted, these may seem like cult magazines, but these publications' circulation numbers are in the millions. *Runner's World* alone has a readership of over 427,000. If you browse its pages, you will find countless articles about ordinary people and their "personal bests." A good barometer of interest in achievement is entering a road race; and according to *Runner's World,* the number of certified road races has tripled since 1984.

Like it or not, the American lifestyle has lost some of its ability to reinforce the achievement motive, and people have turned to sport and recreation for their rewards. If your job gives you a merit increase once a year, and if you only feel success when your son graduates from college, what do you do in the meantime to satisfy your achievement need? Find out by visiting your local health club. Start by examining the new technology. Rather than just bells and whistles, it now provides computerized panels that create instant feedback on your efforts. At the end of an exercise session, you are presented with displays of how hard you worked, how many calories you burned, the distance covered, and your time in motion. If you choose, some machines even give you an imaginary competitor to motivate you during your workout. Look closer and you will see people making notes in personal diaries. It's self-praise—a way of rewarding a job well done. As L.A. fitness watcher Neil Feineman sees it, "We are well beyond the idea of exercise for long-term health. Now fitness is seen as an ideal forum for testing and pushing one's personal limits."

Interpreting Your Score

Fitness scientists Peter and Lorna Francis believe that goal setting in exercise may be important for all of us. They recommend setting goals to help develop a lifetime commitment to exercise. The system they advocate is known as S.M.A.R.T., representing these key dimensions of exercise goals:

S = specific

M = measurable

A = action-oriented

R = realistic

T = timed

If you scored high (7 or above) on the Achievement Quiz, you should take particular note of the S.M.A.R.T. system—you thrive on self-challenge, and this approach to goal-setting will be invaluable. You need to set your mark high, and go for it. You may not care what others do—it is your own standard you try to better. High achievers won't be satisfied unless there is a way of measuring progress. It's likely to be more gratifying if you can see the mileage build up while the time to completion drops. Feedback keeps you motivated whether you are cycling, swimming, rowing, or running. Where there isn't a clock or some other kind of calibration, personal feedback from a coach or a peer will be invaluable.

High achievers should be careful about going full-out when their life stress is high. If you are in a high-stress life situation, setting high fitness goals may increase your chances of injury. This may come about because you are distracted or because you are less tuned in to your body as a result of all the stresses you're experiencing.

What about low scores (3 or less)? Your score could be low for at least two reasons. On the one hand, you might not care to be challenged in life. Feedback about your performance may seem irrelevant. If this is the case, you will probably be satisfied by activities that don't have clear goals or standards. Activities like swimming or rollerblading that lend themselves to self-defined performance standards will do just fine. Fun-filled aerobics classes will also suit you.

On the other hand, you may score low because you shrink from personal challenges. Feedback about your performance may be threatening. If this is the case, the fitness arena is a good place to build up your success rate and to learn how to comfortably confront challenge. You need to start out with reasonable goals, being clear with yourself that you have an objective in mind each time you work out. Make progress notes of your achievements. From time to time, build in a reward—like a new aerobics outfit or a stopwatch for your workouts. As you improve, keep your goals reasonable. Increase the difficulty of your objectives a bit at a time. Make sure the sense of enjoyment remains part of your plan. In time, you will smile instead of grimace when someone confronts you with a challenging situation.

The aim of exercise is to keep at it in a way that satisfies your needs. If you need to be challenged, exercise offers endless opportunity. If you want to avoid personal tests, there are ample non-goal-oriented exercise options to satisfy you.

Kirk worked in industrial relations at a large food-processing plant. Labor-management relations had never been very good, and in the 15 years Kirk had spent on the job, his declining spirit served as a barometer of the slow erosion of trust between the company and its employees. More and more, he felt like a dog chasing his tail. He had always enjoyed the challenge of a new project or a problem that others couldn't solve, but with increasing legislation, his hands were often tied and his mouth gagged. Kirk liked staying fit. As the years passed, he turned more to sport for satisfactions he could no longer derive from work. He said it wasn't competition that drove him, but the need to challenge himself. The technique was simple. He kept a diary of his workouts on his home computer, and at age 41 he took deep satisfaction in the fact that he was lifting heavier weights and running faster times than he had at 35.

Moods and Tension Quiz

Answer Each Question YES, NO, or IN BETWEEN
(Y = Yes   N = No   I = In between)

_____ 1. I am an anxious person.

_____ 2. I suffer from feeling blue or depressed.

_____ 3. My body feels tense a lot of the time.

_____ 4. People who know me think I'm a moody person.

_____ 5. I worry a lot.

Scoring: Give yourself 2 points for "yes" answers, 1 point for "in between" answers, and 0 points for "no" answers. Total your points for questions 1 through 5.

Your score = _____ (0 to 10 points)

Your Mood and Tension Levels

The two emotions most studied by exercise scientists are anxiety and depression. An estimated 8 million Americans suffer from serious clinical depression. Although this amounts to only 3% of the population, the figure doesn't take into account the millions who suffer from depressive feelings of a less severe, but nonetheless disturbing, nature. Anxiety disorders are even more extensive. In fact, they are the most prevalent of all psychological disorders, affecting as many as 24 million adult Americans at some point in their lives. Anxiety assumes many forms, including incessant worry, insomnia, and bodily tension.

The fitness boom has been bolstered by advocates of the mood-tranquilizing benefits of regular exercise. In a 1987 survey by editors of *The Physician and Sportsmedicine*, 82% of the 500 primary care physicians polled regularly prescribed exercise to depressed or anxious patients.

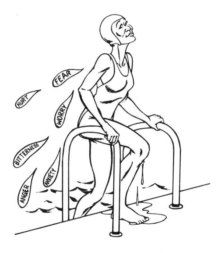

"CLEANSE YOURSELF!"

Personal testimonials about exercise have been replaced by solid research evidence bearing out the belief that you feel better—emotionally—after exercising. The consensus of hundreds of studies is that you get a mood lift when you exercise. It's more reliable than the elusive "runner's high." You are almost certain to feel better after a rigorous workout, even though it may not feel like a peak experience.

The actual mood lift you get from exercise may last only for a few hours before it slips into a more generalized feeling of well-being. By creating the mood lift for yourself through exercise, you gain a sense of personal control over your moods. You learn what you need to do to help manage your emotions. And best of all, the high you get is completely natural.

Tension and anxiety respond about the same way. They dissipate through exercise. You may feel all keyed up before an aerobics class or an evening run, but somewhere in the middle of exercising you lose yourself a little. And then a little more. By the end, you may not have solved the problems that triggered your tension and anxiety, but at least you gave yourself a break with benefits to mind and body.

Psychologists and medical scientists have tried to identify the exact reasons why exercise reduces anxiety. Chemical explanations like the beta-endorphin hypothesis and psychological ones like the "stress reducing time-out" compete for the honors, but whatever the reason, the effect seems to come as an integral part of the exercise package. If you exercise, you will feel less tense. The tension may build up again, but regular exercise helps you manage it.

William Morgan, recent president of the American Psychological Association's Division of Exercise and Sport Psychology, sums it up: "I would like to suggest that running should be viewed as a wonder drug, analogous to penicillin, morphine, and tricyclics. It has a profound potential in preventing mental and physical disease and in rehabilitation after various diseases have occurred."

Although Dr. Morgan's remarks singled out running, I am sure he would agree that equal benefits come with any good aerobic exercise program, including swimming, cycling, dance, calisthenics, and aerobics.

Interpreting Your Score

If you scored high (7 or above) on the Moods and Tension Quiz, you are a prime candidate for a good aerobic exercise program. If your score is low (3 or below), you will still enjoy the benefits of mood elevation and relaxation from exercise, but these will not be your driving reasons to develop the exercise habit.

What's the best exercise program for high scorers? I would like to offer two recommendations. The first is consistent with conclusions from most research on the topic. It is that vigorous exercise that gets your heart beating at about 75% to 80% of the recommended maximum for your age and that is sustained for 20 to 30 minutes should produce a mood boost and a lowering of anxiety. How do you know what's 75% to 80% of your maximum? The general formula has two steps (the example is for a 40-year-old):

1. Subtract your age from the number 220.

$$220 - 40 = 180$$

2. Multiply the result (in this case 180) by .80, which represents 80%.

$$180 \times .80 = 144$$

This 80% value is the number of heartbeats per minute you should have throughout this 20- to 30-minute exercise period.

If all this seems complicated, there are easy-to-use charts you can find in health clubs and book stores that will help you determine your 75%-to-80% value. The more important consideration here is knowing that this means pretty strenuous aerobic exercise. Because aerobic means "oxygen-fueled," you have a wide choice of activities that can keep you huffing and puffing continuously for 20 or more minutes—dancing, swimming, running, skating, and so on.

The problem is, until you get into an exercise routine, you may not feel you have energy enough to exercise, especially when you are a bit down or strung out with anxiety. This is where my second recommendation comes in. I believe that any increase in your general activity level will help if you suffer from mood and tension problems. And it doesn't have to be the huff-and-puff variety of exercise. Don't trap yourself with the belief that you have to exercise to some gasping extreme in order to help yourself emotionally. Although studies do show that anxiety reduction comes most reliably from intense exercise periods of 20 to 30 minutes, we can also affect our moods by getting out of our heads and into our bodies, if only for a few minutes. This could mean getting out of your chair and going for a walk around the block. It might mean doing some deep breathing exercises or some easy stretches.

If you always wait until you feel like doing it, the time may never come. Prepare yourself and remember to make it simple. Learn a 5-minute stretch routine. Find someone to teach you yoga breathing techniques for clearing your mind and energizing yourself. Make an agreement to take periodic 5-minute walks. Then, implement your plan. At least once a day, carry through—stretch, breathe, or walk. Do it again when you feel your energy or mood flagging. Get in the habit. These brief exercise breaks may not produce the more dramatic effects of longer, more strenuous exercise, but they are wonderful nonetheless. They help change your frame of mind and put you in a more positive relation to your body.

After years of psychotherapy, Barney was aware. He knew he got depressed. He even had a good idea why. Some of the newer antidepressants on the market promised relief. He had tried the drug Prozac for about a year with only minimal improvement. He was beyond feeling ashamed about being down so often. He just wanted to feel better, not euphoric, just better than *down*. He enjoyed the outdoors and wondered whether a daily regimen of walking might help. It did—a little. After a few months of walking, he joined a hiking club that advocated daily training walks and keeping up a brisk pace on its biweekly outings. Barney became intrigued by some of the newer techniques and began practicing speed-walking in his neighborhood. It looked funny, but he liked it. A year later he said, "I'm not cured. . . . I probably will never be, but I don't feel as if I'm *under* my emotions any more. I just feel stronger."

Stress Quiz

Answer Each Question YES, NO, or IN BETWEEN
(Y = YES   N = No   I = In between)

_____ 1. My work is *very* stressful.

_____ 2. There have been a lot of changes in my life over the past 12 months.

_____ 3. My life *rarely* feels even and relaxed.

_____ 4. I have to cope with a lot of pressure on a daily basis.

_____ 5. In the past year, I have felt "burned out" by stress.

Scoring: Give yourself 2 points for "yes" answers, 1 point for "in between" answers, and 0 points for "no" answers. Total your points for questions 1 through 5.

Your score = _____ (0 to 10 points)

Managing Your Stress

Stress is an epidemic in modern life. It's a disease of extremes—either you have too much or too little. Psychologists say understimulation can stress us just as much as overstimulation. If you don't believe it, try unemployment for a year. The late Dr. Hans Selye characterized the dilemma by calling stress "the spice of life" and, at the same time, "the wear and tear of life." Selye went so far as to say no one died of old age. To him every death was related to the stress of life. With such a definition, we should all be motivated to manage stress better.

Where this argument breaks down is in the realization that two people will experience the same situation as unequally stressful. One may love to fly, the other may be terrified of air travel. Ultimately, then, stress is reduced to a perception—how you and I interpret reality. In the early 1960s, Dr. Thomas Holmes from the University of Washington's School of Medicine came up with a comprehensive list of life stresses, such as death, divorce, disease, and debt—a modern rendition of the Four Horsemen of the Apocalypse. These stresses were given point values, and the more of these stressful events we experienced in the past year, the more at risk we were thought to be on emotional and physical levels. Oddly enough, some people survived major life stresses, whereas others succumbed to relatively minor ones. The formula needed adjustment.

Newer models of stress management take into account the resources we have to cope with life's demands. Assessing how vulnerable we are to stress now requires information about such factors as health habits, financial status, and supportive relationships in families and friends. They also acknowledge that because of each person's unique history, we may react strongly to situations that others see as benign.

"HOW DO YOU SPELL RELIEF?" "E-X-E-R-C-I-S-E."

In helping people with stress, psychologists work on different levels. One approach is education—assisting people in understanding the stress reaction or helping them change perceptions of events so they appear less threatening. Another approach is lifestyle change. Oftentimes the habits we have developed make it impossible to dissipate stress buildups. Poor eating habits, addictions to drugs, alcohol, or tobacco, and the lack of physical exercise have been targeted as major contributors to stress.

Because stress is ubiquitous, its treatment has to be multifaceted. The unique contribution of exercise to stress management comes from its multidimensionality. Incorporating an exercise program in your life gives you physical, emotional, and social relief. How does it work on a physical level? When the brain receives a "stress signal," heart rate speeds up, blood pressure rises, breathing quickens, and blood rushes to the muscles. The body is preparing to fight or flee danger. Exercise is the best way to use up this rush of stress energy.

In a preventive view, exercise is the best way to toughen the body to respond to life's inevitable stressors and to return to a normal resting state in the shortest time possible. According to Lee Berk, professor of pathology and laboratory medicine at Loma Linda University School of Medicine, exercise becomes a way to practice for stress. "We appear to tune ourselves up by endorphin release. . . . Regular exercisers have frequent practice in releasing endorphins in the proper amount and in the proper patterns to handle stress. When a well-conditioned individual is then exposed to distress, the body responds with practiced efficiency."

Emotional release happens in at least two ways. Exercise works better than commonly prescribed sedatives for calming you down emotionally, according to Herbert de Vries, exercise physiologist and professor emeritus, University of Southern California. It can also provide a more positive release for emotional buildups, and more positive feelings derived from having fun can supplant negative emotions. At the very least, mental worry can be disrupted as you switch your attention from problems to playing a game or enjoying your body.

A third aspect of the exercise benefit to stress management comes through the social networks we develop in fitness. One of the most crucial elements in managing stress is a strong social support network. Dr. Robert Kahn of the University of Michigan likened it to a cargo ship traversing the Atlantic during World War II. If the ship was alone, it didn't have much of a chance; if it was surrounded by a convoy of defending warships, its chances increased dramatically. When we are alone in life, we are more vulnerable to stress. Having friends at the gym or on the running track broadens your support base in times of emotional turmoil.

Interpreting Your Score

Low scores (3 or less) on the Stress Quiz indicate you are handling stress well or that you aren't feeling burdened by life's demands. High scores (7 or more) mean the opposite.

If your Stress Quiz score is 7 or higher, you need to give strong consideration to an exercise program for physical and psychological health reasons. It may well be that if your stress level is this high, you already participate in an exercise program. If you're not exercising, you no doubt will say something like, "I have *no* time!" You may be right, but then you may be suffering from exercise myopia—or the inability to see the opportunities for exercise in your daily schedule.

A friend of mine told me that a year ago his workdays averaged over 11 hours. Now I see him at the health club every day at about 5:30 p.m. Some days he comes twice, once before work and again at the end of the day. He says he gets more done now than he ever did. The explanation? He attributes it to more efficient work habits and having more energy.

Another person I know grumbled that she didn't have the time or energy to work out because she had two small children at home. It took more than a little convincing to have her accept the idea that maybe her husband should take care of the kids a couple evenings a week while she took a yoga class.

Last example. A busy executive ordered a large-screen monitor for her office computer and read off the latest memos, updates, and business data while pedaling her stationary bike. She had mounted a keyboard by the handlebars and got in a good hour of exercise each day while clearing her desk.

Creativity. Part of the answer lies in seeing things differently and not being locked into the "I can't" syndrome. One of life's many ironies is that people who are most in need of something are the least likely to do whatever it is they need. Another is that if you are highly stressed, once you start exercising regularly, you will have difficulty understanding how you ever lived without it.

Here's one more argument for exercise. There have been changes in modern professionals' beliefs about what is the "best" technique for stress management. Ten years ago, relaxation methods and meditation tapes were considered a must for the harried executive. Today, these approaches are still considered valid, but they are not thought to be totally adequate to the task of getting stress under control. Research by psychologist Richard Dienstbier, a professor at the University of Nebraska, supports a growing belief that we have to toughen ourselves to master the stresses in our daily lives. According to Dienstbier, hard aerobic workouts may be one of the best methods available. If we never learn to stand face to face with adversity, we may be doomed to dwell in our emotional miasmas. Flexing muscles and getting physically tough transfer to real-world encounters where we have to stand our ground and face the paper tigers that assail us.

Sheila was a fifth-grade math teacher in an inner-city school. As was true of most cities across the country, the inner core had deteriorated badly since the sixties. The children she taught typically were troubled and difficult. The noise level in the school in itself was almost too much to deal with, but adding on the threats, violence, and drug-related crime left Sheila rattled at the end of most workdays. Going home right after school to her own noisy household was the last thing she wanted to do. She needed a retreat, a place that was hers where she could let go. The local health club offered little respite. Speakers blared nonstop mind-numbing rock-and-roll, and the jumble of bodies and machines made her even more tense and irritable. She had taken ballet as a young girl, and it was in this ritualistic exercise that she found her haven. With classical music in the background, she could focus on her movements and feel a sense of control returning to her body and mind.

Search for Meaning Quiz

Answer Each Question YES, NO, or IN BETWEEN
(Y = Yes   N = No   I = In between)

_____ 1. I feel something important is missing in my life.

_____ 2. I often wonder what my life is all about.

_____ 3. When I take time to reflect, I feel troubled by the shallowness of my lifestyle.

_____ 4. There seems to be a deeper purpose to life that I have difficulty connecting to.

_____ 5. I sometimes fear that as my life is ending I will realize I have completely missed its point.

Scoring: Give yourself 2 points for "yes" answers, 1 point for "in between" answers, and 0 points for "no" answers. Total your points for questions 1 through 5.

Your score = _____ (0 to 10 points)

The Search for Meaning

We thought we had it in the sixties, we hung onto it for a while in the seventies, and then we crashed into the abyss in the eighties. Now, in the nineties, we feel lost, but at least that's a start.

Whether it was the Vietnam war, racism, or sexism that we were fighting, we had a purpose in the sixties. There was an enemy of one sort or another, and that made it easy. But then, more and more, the bad guys became ubiquitous, they became us; and so in the seventies we purged our conscience in encounter groups and consciousness-raising sessions until we felt the harmony of universal oneness in the human struggle.

In the eighties, we put all this aside and got down to business. MBAs supplanted psychology degrees as the hot ticket to happiness. Careers in medicine plummeted in popularity as concerns about liability outstripped considerations of human welfare. We were into money and the lifestyles it could provide. Status was no longer writing poetry and singing songs of protest, but the Mont Blanc pen you owned, irrespective of whether you ever used it. The emphasis was on ownership—and as the designer T-shirt proclaimed, "He who dies with the most toys WINS."

The vacuousness of our pursuits was aptly expressed in a New Yorker cartoon depicting an obviously successful man leaning against his sports car and lamenting, "I despise my life, but I'm in love with my lifestyle." God died somewhere around 1966, according to *Time* magazine, and so for the next decade we patched together a new moral network with the aid of gurus, shamans, and psychologist-priests. The foundations of our new morality were crumbling long before the scandals of evangelists Jim Bakker and Jimmy Swaggart. The Jonestown mass suicide was perhaps our clearest omen of the danger of placing faith in man and artifacts of our egos. It was "The Big Chill."

The dilemma was how to look within while the glitter of life became ever more seductive. Money became our god, and the more you had, the more you were worshipped. Donald Trump grew bigger than life. He didn't have to jump tall buildings in a single bound. He bought them and put his name on them instead. Our valuation of him had nothing to do with whether he had extramarital affairs, but with how much he could entertain us with his flamboyance. As churches tried to reassert their relevance in modern life amidst the AIDS epidemic and signs of our decadence, countless priests and ministers were charged with sexually abusing their young altar boys and boarding-school charges. It was "game over."

As Lawrence Shames, author and former ethics columnist for *Esquire*, described the eighties: "The beginning of this decade saw something basic being distanced, repackaged, made into something to be looked at rather than embraced. . . . It was called life. . . . Or rather, it used to be called life, until people realized you could charge more for it if you called it *lifestyle*." In his book, *The Hunger for More: Searching for Values in an Age of Greed*, Shames notes that our fascination with lifestyles was fine "as long as the stores were open, as long as the restaurants were serving, as long as there was someplace to go in the car." But our obsession with lifestyle in lieu of life advanced only by substituting false needs for true ones, and "it conquered, finally, by making of itself not a set of chosen pleasures but an addiction." The conflict materialized in a battle of time versus money. There weren't enough hours in the day for it all, so what became expendable were things like friendship and romance. Like sitting around and wondering about life's mysteries. And like the private inner things whose value you alone determined.

And where did exercise fit into all of this? According to Shames, if exercise became part of the lifestyle, it highlighted only what you could see. It was "a matter of silhouette, the outline of one's flesh in the mirrors of the aerobics room." Unfortunately, this became a moralistic complaint that cemented many into sedentary lifestyles. Fitness was for narcissists. There was no intrinsic value in its pursuit. Indeed, when surveys appeared on reasons people exercised, two of the highest ranked values were "to look better" and "to lose weight."

What was missed in this snapshot analysis of the fitness world was how people were subtly transformed by their pursuit of the ideal physical profile. A survey conducted by *Runner's World* in 1989 showed that psychological benefits of exercise motivated only about 40% of beginning runners, but after getting involved in their programs nearly 80% subscribed to the mental health benefits of exercise.

The depth of this transformation in values is only hinted at by statistics. In describing the meaning derived from exercise, George Leonard, author of *The Ultimate Athlete*, philosophized that exercise's "total discharge of the body involves a surrender of the ego that is akin to dying. In this surrender, this sense of death and rebirth, there is health and exaltation." Thaddeus Kostubala, psychiatrist and the author of *The Joy of Running*, notes: "I've seen runners change their jobs, their living areas, their marital status, even their religion. . . . Especially as the mileage goes up, the brain undergoes phenomenal stimulation. The changes in women are even more striking than in men—it's almost as if they have been unshackled." And perhaps most poetically, we find the deeper dimensions of exercise venerated in the words of Robert Louis Stevenson: "[Exercise] . . . that fine intoxication that comes of much motion in the open air, that begins in a sort of dazzle and sluggishness of the brain, and ends in a peace that passes all understanding."

Interpreting Your Score

If you scored high (7 or more) on the Search for Meaning Quiz, you may be skeptical about finding your life's purpose in a gym or on a runner's path. And for this reason, it becomes essential to distinguish means from ends. The act of exercising is only the vehicle that holds potential for bringing you to these profound discoveries. Yes, you can also do it by sitting quietly in meditation or by going to church and praying. Yet exercise is unique in what it offers our quest.

As with any means, exercise can be misguided. If what you seek is knowing a deeper purpose in life, you won't find it pursuing increased muscular definition or higher aerobic performance. You certainly won't find it obsessing about how much body fat gets squeezed between skinfold calipers. It comes, as does happiness, through your being present to yourself and receptive to its arrival. The biochemical edge provided by exercise's endorphin release may serve as one of the keys that opens your mind to your inner self.

Scientists might talk about it differently, but it comes down to the same thing. Studying brain function, they note an alteration in our brain wave patterns. Here we would call this consciousness. In the repetitive movements of exercise, our minds seem to jump tracks, switching back and forth from left-brain to right-brain functioning. This added benefit is provided by few other personal pursuits.

In a simpler sense, exercise can be an intensely personal time that permits reflection on all that we value, yearn for, and love. The tranquility that emerges through a long run or swim makes it easier somehow to face ourselves squarely and ponder the meanings in our lives. At the very least, if you experience an inner void, giving yourself space and time for self-discovery will help. The secret is that it's already there, waiting to be known and brought fully into your life.

Low scores on this quiz (3 or below) suggest you have found an inner harmony based on a sense of purpose in your life. This doesn't mean exercise is irrelevant to your needs, but rather that other factors will serve as stronger motivators. Even so, knowing your purpose and spending time with it in private exercise might be additionally revealing.

The "runner's high" has often been described in quasi-mystical, spiritual ways. Dr. Ari Kiev, who directs the Life Strategy Workshop in New York City, advocates running and such unorthodox exercises as swimming alongside dolphins to help us achieve this deep, inner feeling. His reasons? "We live in an extremely materialistic world in which great emphasis is placed on external performance, and the soul underneath is forgotten. Running is one way to help get beneath the masks we all wear. We spend much of our lives covering up our vulnerabilities and insecurities. Running is a way of getting back in touch with who we really are." (*The Runner*, March 1987, p. 34)

Playfulness Quiz

Answer Each Question YES, NO, or IN BETWEEN
(Y = Yes   N = No   I = In between)

_____ 1. I consider myself to be a playful person.

_____ 2. People tell me I am fun to be with.

_____ 3. I like to play games and sports just for the fun of it.

_____ 4. My sense of humor is one of my most valued assets.

_____ 5. I have an easy time getting into a playful spirit.

Scoring: Give yourself 2 points for "yes" answers, 1 point for "in between" answers, and 0 points for "no" answers. Total your points for questions 1 through 5.

Your score = _____ (0 to 10 points)

How Playful Are You?

What does it mean to be playful? Is it acting childlike? Is it being a practical joker? Or is it being lighthearted and ready to laugh? There are people we know who make us smile. They have an infectious humor. They like to play. Even while working, they have a good time. It's Murray Burns in "A Thousand Clowns," Lucille Ball in "I Love Lucy," or Ruth Gordon in "Harold and Maude." Maybe it's Peter Falk in "Columbo" or Kato in "The Pink Panther." You know it when you see it, because you remember. As a child you knew instinctively what it was when you chased a kite or pumped on a swing until you almost touched the sky.

But something happened. We became too serious. Life closed in, and even the lighter moments get colored by tragedy and loss. The role played by John Candy in "Planes, Trains, and Automobiles" is a perfect example of the funny man masking sadness. It's hard for us to enjoy slapstick without seeing the violence, or to listen to some humor without feeling its veiled hostility. The legacy of Freudianism and our enlightened times? Perhaps. Or maybe we are reacting to a growing disillusionment over having tried to achieve Hollywood endings in our own lives but having suffered instead reality's inevitable slap.

It's fine to analyze laughter and play at philosophical levels, as long as we retain the ability to appreciate them concretely in our lives. Norman Cousins, in his runaway bestseller *The Anatomy of an Illness*, described the healing powers of laughter. In his journey back to health from a terminal illness, Cousins locked himself in a room with reels of comedy films. He literally laughed himself back to health.

It may seem odd to be talking about exercise in the same context as play. Indeed, this misconception is one of the travesties of the fitness movement. To be fit, we are advised to walk stairs instead of taking elevators, to sit on stationary bikes, or to do aerobics in front of a television screen. This isn't wrong, it just isn't the whole picture. There are other choices.

If exercise is continually portrayed as exhausting, painful, or difficult, we collectively lose something. For all of us, there have to be ways of increasing the degree of playfulness in our adult years. Joyless exercise repeated as a daily ritual dampens the spirit. Even if it is only a playful attitude that we bring to exercise, the benefits we reap from letting our inner child out are immeasurable.

Committing yourself to exercise can be serious business. Setting goals, scheduling time, and going to classes take determination, and sometimes that sounds the death knell for fun. Indeed, according to sportswriter Ellen Steinbaum, commenting in *Self* magazine, the missing ingredient "is what physical activity meant as a child—pleasure. A child doesn't run because it is a sensible way to stay healthy and fit; she does it because it's fun. Seeking out and savoring pleasure is the key to relearning the lost enjoyment of living in one's body." The message couldn't have been clearer to me than it was this past Christmas. I had enticed my family into a brisk walk on the frozen lake in front of our Laurentian cottage. It was about –20 degrees Celsius. Real cold! We had been cooped up most of the day, and I was in the mood for some exercise. I led the march onto the ice. After

"PLAY BALL? YOU KIDDIN'? MY TEAM'S UP AT BAT!"

about 10 minutes, I became aware that I was spending more time hounding my kids to keep up the pace than enjoying a little aerobic activity.

My son, Jacob, the skateboarder-snowboarder-basketball-player but definitely-not-runner, pronounced those much feared but all-powerful adolescent words: "I'm bored!" In exasperation, I said, "So, what do you want to do?" Without missing a beat, he responded, "How about a game of tic-tac-toe?" In an incredulous voice, I answered, "Where? Here? On the ice?" He didn't wait. Jake's feet were shuffling in the fresh powder that covered the ice, making lines up and down and across. My daughter Susannah, the rollerblader-basketball-player-swimmer, was busy making her lines in the snow. Two 10-foot tic-tac-toe games had been drawn on the ice, and the only thing left was to decide who went first.

The games slid into snow design contests, snow scribblings, and a predictable chase called, "Let's catch dad and stuff snow down his neck." I got my aerobic workout. The kids were ecstatic. As we collapsed in front of the fire for some hot chocolate, I realized I had become so locked into my patterns of exercising that I had lost touch with its purpose. Sure, it's great to be strong and fit so you can move couches during spring cleaning and run to catch the bus, but what about being "fit for fun"? The opportunity had to penetrate layers of preconceptions and habit for me to see what was so obvious. *Being playful is both the means and the end of being fit.*

Interpreting Your Score

Depending on your score on the Playfulness Quiz, your agenda may be to learn more about your playful side or to nurture what you already value. The idea of rote calisthenics may be anathema to the playful spirit, but for this same person a good game of volleyball would be like an ice cream wagon's bells to a child's ears. If you scored 7 or higher on the quiz, you may retreat from exercise where grimaces and groans outnumber peals of laughter. You may be drawn more to activities with gamelike qualities where people are lighthearted rather than heavy-footed.

It's true that some activities draw out your playful spirit more than others. A game of volleyball may be more fun than running on a treadmill. Unfortunately, it may be hard to find a volleyball game three or more times a week. What you may need to do is identify your ingredients for fun. It might be doing things with a friend. Or it could be making sure there's variety in what you do. Perhaps there's a way you like to make games out of things. Bringing these elements into your fitness program will help keep it enjoyable.

If your score is low (3 or less), do you feel you are missing something? Would you like to be more playful? Is there a reluctant child inside that has to be coaxed to join in the fun? If you have some suspicions that the serious side of your nature has taken over, consider getting some practice in playfulness. Make a deal with yourself to join a volleyball league. Go to a roller rink and take a few spins. Treat yourself to windsurfing lessons. Or maybe just invite yourself out for a night of dancing.

Maybe he picked it up from his father. Gene's dad had a trunk full of magic tricks, a basement overflowing with model trains, and even a little puppet theater that he set up on the lawn in summertime to entertain neighborhood kids. Gene's childhood was filled with warm, noisy spasms of laughter and family pillow fights. Even chores were playfully designed—like shuffling on wooden floors with oversized socks to buff the sweet-smelling wax. Grade-school teachers described him as a "joyful learner" who asked the most profound questions with wide-eyed wonder. Sure, he also had a reputation as class clown.

His school friends always looked to him when things got boring. He could devise new games on the spur of the moment. He intuitively understood how to make things interesting. As he entered his thirties, most of his friends were joining health clubs for recreation. Gene thought there had to be another way. He read about "new games and sports," those creative, noncompetitive activities that anyone can play. Then, he designed a program for his local community center. It was called "Playtime for Big Kids." You never knew what was going to happen when you arrived at the center, but you could be sure Gene had dreamed up something fun. Maybe it was an adult version of hide-and-seek or musical chairs. As you were leaving the center, you might hear him yelling, "Anybody around my base is it!"

Reviewing Your Psychological Motives

Psychological motives derive from things you have inside you—emotions and feelings—that determine how you experience yourself in the world. Whether you are playful or stressed-out affects what you do and how you do it. Similarly, if you suffer from low self-esteem or persistent anxiety, you may shy away from potentially rewarding situations in life. These dimensions of your character are interrelated. No doubt, if you get your emotions under control, your self-esteem will increase. If you feel less stressed, you might even feel a little playful on occasion. Exercise programs offer solid benefits to your psychological well-being. It's important to consider which exercise suits you best for the things you need most, but the general guideline is to get involved.

The next chapter, on social motives, focuses on other dimensions of your character and approach to life. You may find parallels between your psychological and social motives. The importance of viewing the social motives in light of your knowledge of your scores on the psychological motives is to help you fine-tune your self-analysis and to determine what kind of exercise programs will work best for you.

Completing Your Profile

A graph is provided in Figure 4.1 so you can create a visual overview of your scores. This is similar to the one you completed in chapter 3. Write your six psychological motive scores in the spaces provided on the graph. On the left side of the graph, you will find a scale ranging from 0 to 10. Start with your score on the Self-Esteem Quiz. Draw a line corresponding to your score (0 to 10) across the top of the Self-Esteem column. Then shade in the area in the column beneath the line. Do the same for the other motives.

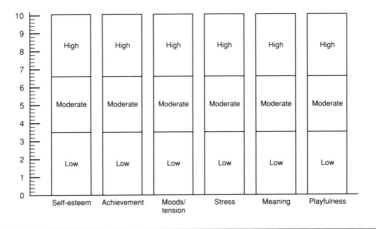

Figure 4.1   In the graph above, each column represents one of the six psychological motives. For each, draw a line corresponding to your score across the column, then shade in the area below your line.

The Psychological Motives Profile you have just created will help you compare your six scores. You can determine which is your highest and lowest. If your psychological motives are uniformly high, it will call your attention to the potency of these motives for supporting an exercise habit. Conversely, if they are uniformly low, it means you may have to look to other motives to reinforce an exercise program.

Take a few minutes to consider what this graph says about you. Question yourself about your reactions to this profile. Does it make sense to you? Does it accurately portray who you are? Do you feel good about it? Make notes on your reactions so you have a record of any things you might want to emphasize or change as you go about designing an exercise program in later chapters.

CHAPTER 5

YOUR SOCIAL MOTIVES AND HOW TO USE THEM

"No man is an island, entire of itself; every man is a piece of the continent, a part of the main."
JOHN DONNE

Do you

- want to make friends who share your energy?
- need a safe way of blowing off steam?
- have trouble asserting yourself?
- want to sharpen your competitive edge?
- want to even out relationship highs and lows?
- need to take charge of your life?

A "yes" answer to any of these questions means exercise can provide the key to satisfying your social motives. How this can happen will be described in the sections below.

What Are Your Social Motives?

Sport and exercise have long been valued for their socializing effects. They bring people together with a common purpose. We encourage young children to play games with others as a way to learn social and cooperative behavior. However, a different social emphasis emerges when winning becomes the agenda. Competition is one of life's lessons, but if winning is its sole objective, social aggression is likely to soar.

Anger and aggression go together, and though aggressive behavior may be necessary for survival, problems occur when we are too aggressive or are not aggressive enough. We either express it too openly, hurting those around us, or we don't express it well enough, keeping it in and hurting ourselves.

If we express too much anger, we must learn constructive ways to rid ourselves of this destructive emotion. If we keep anger in, we must learn how to be more assertive, to release the anger, and to prevent more from building up. Exercise can provide a safe outlet for built-up frustrations and teach us how to be more assertive.

Another aspect of social life involves intimate personal relationships. Some people ride relationship roller-coasters, feeling out of control when relationships break up or hit turbulent times. When this happens, it may be difficult getting your mind off your troubles long enough to begin healing and discovering new ways of being in relationships.

You may also find it hard to take charge of your life after a relationship turns sour or after a traumatic experience. You need more personal power and self-control. This chapter will examine the role exercise can play in helping you manage relationship swings and gain control over your life.

Sociability Quiz

Answer Each Question YES, NO, or IN BETWEEN
(Y = Yes   N = No   I = In between)

_____ 1. I feel completely at ease at parties and social gatherings.

_____ 2. I have lots of good friends, and I make time to be with them.

_____ 3. I typically make it a point to find people to do things with rather than doing things alone.

_____ 4. I usually feel energized when I spend a lot of time with people.

_____ 5. I have a habit of striking up conversations with complete strangers.

Scoring: Give yourself 2 points for "yes" answers, 1 point for "in between" answers, and 0 points for "no" answers. Total your points for questions 1 through 5.

Your score = _____ (0 to 10 points)

Sociability—How Do You Rate?

Sure, we're social animals, yet we differ in the amount of time we like to spend with others. People who are more inward are often called introverts; those who are more gregarious are often referred to as extroverts. What makes life difficult is that sometimes we have to do things that don't fit our social preferences. We may work in sales and be worn out by constant contact with other people. We may end up in a research lab, working alone but craving company. And, of course, parenthood can turn into a unique form of social deprivation.

Let's take a different angle on sociability. Strong positive social bonds are known to promote physical and psychological well-being. Psychologist David McClelland of Boston University found that feelings that come with loving or being loved are linked with higher levels of antibodies. Just thinking about or being in the presence of a loving person may be enough to elevate levels of lgA antibodies, which are your main line of defense against colds and other upper respiratory infections. Feelings of love and caring for others also seem to reduce stress chemicals in the body. Supporting McClelland's argument, a recent study at the University of Michigan by sociologist James House suggests that a lack of social relationships puts people at greater risk of dying prematurely.

What's the exercise connection? It's twofold. The first part is obvious. We know that the new social scene is centered in the fitness world. Fred LeBow, president of the New York Road Runners Club, recently declared that the 1-1/2 mile loop around the Central Park reservoir has replaced singles bars as the meeting place of choice for many New Yorkers. Even if you aren't looking for a mate, exercise facilities are a good place to meet people. According to Professor Harold Minden of York University in Toronto, many of the reasons people give for sport participation can be interpreted as social ones, including making new friends. And usually you are off on the right foot with an interest in common—fitness.

The second part is more subtle, but it is probably a more potent force in social bonding. Although this is hard to document, friendships formed through shared fitness involvements tend to be closer and more intimate than those formed otherwise. Why? Perhaps it's because we're sharing something physical. The intensity and struggle of exercise opens us to emotions that we then connect to those who accompany us in fitness rituals. In some instances, it may come through touch—a powerful bonding experience found in many team sports and other group activities.

Interpreting Your Score

If you scored 7 or more on the Sociability Quiz, you like spending time with people. The next question, however, is whether you also have a need to be alone. Fitness offers a world of choices for your social needs. Some high socializers like to take their social nature right into their workouts. Exercising alone would feel like punishment. They arrange to meet someone, run with a partner, or find a friendly game of tennis. Others who are equally sociable use their workouts as private time, a unique opportunity to sort things out by themselves. For them, a solitary run in the park is just what the doctor ordered. It's a way of balancing their personalities.

If you scored 3 or less on the quiz, your social needs are less central. You spend more time alone. There are different reasons for this. You may enjoy your private world and feel indifferent to spending time with others. Or you may be uncomfortable with others, not knowing how to make friends or how to keep them; in this case it isn't exactly a choice to be alone, but rather something you can't seem to change.

Dr. Hans Eysenck, a pioneer in personality measurement, concluded that the trait of introversion-extroversion is biologically based and not subject to change. One implication of his work is if you're an introvert, you're not likely to become extroverted by exercising in a group. But there are other goals than becoming the life of the party. If you tend to be introverted, perhaps exercise can help you achieve reasonable objectives—like strengthening ties with close friends by working out together or learning ways to feel more comfortable in social settings.

How should you design an exercise program based on your score? Low socializers who feel good about the amount of contact they have with others are best advised to find a solitary activity they enjoy—like running, cycling, or swimming. It may come as a surprise that even activities like aerobics can be quite solitary, in that classes don't require interaction.

What if you are unhappy with your social isolation and want to feel more comfortable with others? Exercise offers a unique solution. It has been well established that exercising helps us feel less anxious, not only after we exercise, but while we are doing it. Because anxiety is an emotion that impedes social contact, getting involved in exercise will help. It starts when you decide to work on your social skills while exercising. Next, you have to select activities that connect you with people. For instance, there are running clubs in towns and cities throughout North America. All you have to do is show up—the rest will take care of itself. Participation in the activity will help you manage the emotion of anxiety, and you can gradually work your way into conversations as the motions of running ease your mind into a more comfortable frame. If you don't like running, you can find hiking, cycling, sailing, swimming, or social dancing clubs that make it easy for you to sweat unabashedly while you socialize.

Both high and low scores on the Sociability Test are relevant to the exercise question. Your score directs you in one of two ways: either to cater to your inclinations or to help you change. If the agenda is the status quo, then the choices are obvious—social activities for social people, solitary ones for those who like to guard their private time. If the agenda is change, then the first thing to do is to make up your mind that this is something you want to work on—and commit yourself to it. Compulsively social people may need to work on their inner selves through solitary experiences, and shy or socially anxious people may want to improve their relations with others. Recognize that choosing activities that run against your grain means you may have a harder time keeping to your commitment. Extra attention to your resolution will be necessary to develop the exercise habit.

Beth lived like a hermit. Although she worked as a head nurse in a busy city hospital, once quitting time came she entered a self-imposed isolation ward called home. She allowed work to fill the missing pieces of her life. There was little energy left for anything once she got through with her 10-hour workdays and the project piles she carried home at night. She rarely dated and often thought of herself as a social failure. Although she belonged to a few clubs and went to parties when invited, social outings took their toll. She felt she didn't belong. Her one outlet was swimming. It relaxed her. While doing laps one day, Beth got recruited for a women's swim team. She wanted to say no, but some other part of her blurted out "Yes." The team was good—and members were determined to be number one in the city. They pushed Beth, encouraging her to practice and to participate in swim meets. She was forced to ease off at work and was surprised how quickly she got used to that. By her third season, she was voted team captain. She said jokingly that her social awkwardness just seemed to wash off after a few thousand meters in the pool.

Anger Quiz

Answer Each Question YES, NO, or IN BETWEEN
(Y = Yes   N = No   I = In between)

_____ 1. I lose my temper easily.

_____ 2. I often feel hostility building up inside me.

_____ 3. I am easily irritated by things like poor service or waiting
in lines.

_____ 4. I frequently make cynical or sarcastic comments.

_____ 5. When I'm upset, I have a tendency to say mean things or
do things I am sorry for later on.

Scoring: Give yourself 2 points for "yes" answers, 1 point for "in
between" answers, and 0 points for "no" answers. Total your points
for questions 1 through 5.

Your score = _____ (0 to 10 points)

How Angry Are You?

More than a quarter-century ago, researchers identified a behavior pattern
believed to be linked to coronary heart disease. They called it *Type A
behavior.* It included habits of impatience, setting increasingly difficult
goals, taking on too much work, emphasizing quantity over quality, and
being unable to relax. Millions of research dollars later, the conclusions
of the original work had to be modified. It wasn't the rush-rush, hurry-
hurry pattern that led to heart disease. The killer trait was anger.

According to Dr. Redford Williams, director of the behavioral medicine
research center at Duke University and author of *The Trusting Heart,*
hostility, anger, and their biological consequences are the toxic part
of Type A behavior. Williams puts it bluntly: "Ambition won't kill
you—hostility will." The mechanism, according to Dr. Williams, can be
found in how the heart responds: "Hostile people have more significant
blood pressure responses when they are angry than do non-hostile
people."

People who get angry easily or who report frequent feelings of hostility
are more likely than others to suffer from coronary heart disease. This
well-documented conclusion fits common sense. When we see someone
getting angry, we have a number of expressions that capture the dynamics.

"Hey, don't blow a gasket!" "Better watch your blood pressure!" Or more directly, "Hey buddy, don't have a heart attack!"

Beet-red faces, pulsing arteries, and gritted teeth mark the experience of anger. The last thing an angry person wants to do is to take a few deep breaths to calm down. More likely, he wants to hit something or in some other way physically vent his feelings. Dealing with anger is a complex task. It requires not only getting to the roots of the anger, but finding ways of coping with the feelings when they arise. The danger is one of limiting interventions to those that look for the causes of a person's anger—which may take years of psychotherapy—without creating outlets that provide immediate relief and enable the individual to function with more emotional balance in the moment.

"I COULD HAVE HAD A RUN!"

Interpreting Your Score

You probably don't experience much anger or hostility if you score low (3 or less) on the Anger Quiz. Your exercise connection will likely come from other dimensions of your character. A high score (7 or more), however, indicates your angry emotions get the better of you more than you would like. If you score high, you need ways to safely release emotions that build up in daily life. What's the exercise answer? It's probably not racquetball, although it may be karate. Ideally, it would be something soothing like yoga, but you might have a hard time getting into it. Finding the exercise answer will take a little understanding.

Let's start with information. Anger and hostility are not just psychological states. These emotions have strong physical components—from a racing heart and hypertension to chemical releases in the bloodstream that prepare us for a real battle. We need to purge the body of these emotions and their physiological residue. According to James Blumenthal, associate professor of medical psychology at Duke University, exercise is a great way to do this. In his study, Type A men were able to blunt their exaggerated cardiovascular responses to stress with a regimen of aerobic exercise. Blumenthal does not, however, believe that exercise changes the Type A's attitudes; it just gives them a safety valve to release pressure they create.

Another study, by Dr. Redford Williams of Duke University Medical Center, noted that aerobic exercise improves the response of the vagus nerve, which regulates heart rate. Having a strong vagal response slows the resting heart rate and can protect against sudden death in people who have had heart attacks. A report by Dennis Lobstein, professor of exercise physiology at the University of New Mexico, also indicates that "when anger prone individuals improve their aerobic fitness levels through exercise, their heart and blood pressure responses fall closer to normal range."

What about the type of exercise you do? Carol Tavris, author of *Anger: The Misunderstood Emotion*, believes that exercise can help put some emotional distance between you and the source of your anger. "Exercise may be helpful if it allows you to burn off excess energy without making you more aggressive." So the key is finding activities that allow you to release rather than aggravate angry feelings. Would this mean *no* to tennis and golf?

Consider the logic before answering. There are two problem areas. First, an activity that has winners and losers or that requires great skill to perform can be frustrating to participants. On a good day, it may be fine. But you're not always at your best, and when you most need a release, you may be confronted with additional aggravation by losing or performing poorly.

The second problem derives from what psychologists refer to as "social learning." Behaviors we practice get reinforced. When we play aggressive sports, what social behaviors do we learn? Aggressive ones, of course. And what effect might this have? Well, according to good evidence, it increases the chances we will act aggressively.

Martial arts may be an exception. This kind of training, with a good instructor, emphasizes mastery of emotions, learning to meditate, and quieting the mind. It takes time and commitment, but the rewards come in proportion to your efforts. According to a recent study at Carleton University by Dr. T. A. Nosenchuk, martial arts training results in a decrease rather than an increase in aggressiveness over time.

What if you can't do martial arts? There are other activities that can help. Many runners insist they release angry feelings by screaming into the wind or converting anger's energy into a full-out sprint. Weight lifters make similar claims. They talk about venting their frustrations on the machines or on free weights. They describe it in terms like "soul cleansing," "rejuvenating," or simply "taking the edge off." Remember, you don't want to choose an activity that may nurture anger or frustration. Golf and racquet sports score high in this respect. Sure it may feel good to smash a ball over the net, but what if you hit the net? Choose an activity where performance isn't the goal. Depending on your self-diagnosis, you may be able to slide right into a daily routine of yoga that keeps you feeling relaxed and unkinked. Maybe yoga is too passive for your tastes and you need a more active outlet. Aerobics would be a good choice—provided you don't have too many problems learning choreography. If you do, it may be another frustration that causes your blood to boil. You may have to try out a few activities to find how you react. If it calms you in the moment and gives you a greater sense of harmony throughout the day, you have your match.

Julia was madder than hell. But she didn't know why. On a day-to-day basis, she could point to hundreds of things that irritated her, but it was evident to her and everyone else that whatever was bugging her wasn't what she was complaining about in the moment. She sought counsel. She raged about her parents on the analyst's couch and pounded them into the floor in primal sessions. It helped for a while, but as soon as she stopped therapy, the feelings came back. She tried meditation, but felt too jumpy—it was excruciating sitting still for half an hour at a time. A friend suggested a more active kind of meditation, an exercise called t'ai chi. It consisted of a choreographed sequence of movements combined with specific mental meditations. She committed herself and learned all the moves in 6 months. From that point on, she was able to do t'ai chi whenever she wanted to, whenever she needed to—including at the office, in the park, at home, or even, she admitted, in the women's restroom. It calmed her down. It was easy, and she could do it every day. In fact, she started the day with it, then she did it before lunch and once again in the evening. It took about 10 minutes each time. Thirty minutes a day. Was it worth it? Julia told her friend, "It's really great—but for those really bad days, I've taken up boxing lessons."

----------------------------------- **Assertiveness Quiz** -----------------------------------

Answer Each Question YES, NO, or IN BETWEEN
(Y = Yes   N = No   I = In between)

_____ 1. I need to be more assertive in how I handle situations.

_____ 2. I feel pushed around by life and too weak to push back.

_____ 3. I avoid returning items to stores for refunds or complaining about bad service in a restaurant.

_____ 4. I have a hard time standing up for myself.

_____ 5. I feel uncomfortable when I make my needs known to others.

Scoring: Give yourself 2 points for "yes" answers, 1 point for "in between" answers, and 0 points for "no" answers. Total your points for questions 1 through 5.

Your score = _____ (0 to 10 points)

How Assertive Are You?

We just finished talking about anger and people who act *too* aggressively, and it might seem logical that if you scored high on anger, you probably wouldn't show up as being unassertive. However, many people who suffer from being overly angry also display characteristics of unassertiveness. Why?

Assertiveness means being able to stand up for your rights comfortably—without apology or anger. If you get poor service, you let it be known in such a way that the situation is rectified without trammeling someone else's rights. It's showing respect for others while acknowledging that you have rights, too.

Oftentimes, when people are unassertive, they let things build up and then explode inappropriately. It's the straw that breaks the camel's back. When you feel unable to assert your needs, pressure builds up. One way or another, it gets expressed. You either blow out or blow in. Blowing out takes the form of anger. Blowing in looks like guilt and depression.

Assertiveness isn't just a verbal skill. It has a body component in how we present ourselves to others and in how we feel inside our skin. Think of a time when you were very anxious about talking to someone or confronting an issue. You might recall the weak-knee syndrome, when your legs felt like jelly. Assertiveness has much to do with feeling strong in your body, of feeling your legs under you while you are asserting yourself.

That's a good lead-in to the exercise connection. Consider the following scenario: You have to make a presentation to a group of rather intimidating individuals. You have to be tough because you know they are going to fight your proposal every inch of the way. From your personal history, you know it's hard to stand up for yourself. You have 2 hours before the meeting, and you can choose one of the following strategies for spending time:

1. You can rehearse your proposal one more time.
2. You can go into a quiet room and meditate.
3. You can take a leisurely swim in a pool.
4. You can work out with weights.

Hard choice? Each answer has possibilities, and depending on your history, the right choice could be any one of the four. However, chances are that strategy #1 would get you overly worried and anxious; strategy #2 would fail because unless you have practiced meditation for a few years, you won't be able to quiet your mind under pressure; strategy #3 would leave you feeling like limp linguini when you meet these folks; and strategy #4 might be just what you need. If you want to feel strong and assertive, what better way to prepare than to get those feelings into your body. Pumping iron makes you feel your strength, giving you the physical sensation of overcoming resistance and matching force with force.

This example speaks to an immediate situation. In reality, you may not have a couple of hours to prepare for each confrontation life throws your way. So, for the long run, what do you do? In the exercise world, you want to do something that builds strength, makes you feel grounded, and takes you out of hiding into the open. Translating this into activities means doing things like racquet sports and lifting weights. Or running sprints instead of passive jogging. Or even taking aerobics, but standing at the front of the class. Partly, it's an attitude of putting yourself out there, of imagining yourself being strong as you move through your workout. And partly, it's choosing a sport where you can sense mastery, where you can pit yourself against an obstacle—like weights or an opponent—and challenge yourself to succeed. It's engaging only sparingly in activities that are passive and yielding, like yoga or easy swimming or easy anything. Sport psychologist Jerry Lynch, from the Center for Optimal Performance in Santa Cruz, found this to be the case with endurance athletes he studied. People who trained for long-distance contests such as marathons or triathlons had the ability to tolerate failure, setbacks, and mistakes. "They're very determined, persistent, patient people," says

Lynch. These traits developed through sport participation are just the qualities called for in an assertive lifestyle.

Claire Schmais, a professor in the dance/movement therapy program at New York's Hunter College, offers support for martial arts training in learning assertive interaction patterns. She believes it teaches "a sensitivity to others, to know when to go for it punch for punch and when to let it go."

The other day, I watched a young woman lackadaisically pedaling a stationary bike while reading a novel. An aggressive man walked over to her and convinced her that she had exceeded the club's 30-minute time limit. In fact, she had been pedaling no more than 20 minutes. She seemed mildly upset and tried to protest, but it was no contest. My armchair character analysis (in fact, I was struggling on the rowing machine) was that if she had been pushing herself to the limit, she might have had other words for this bully.

Interpreting Your Score

Your score? If it's low (3 or less) on the Assertiveness Quiz, you have little difficulty asserting yourself in most situations. An exercise program won't be necessary to build your assertiveness, though it might be helpful in maintaining it. If your score is high (7 or more), you have some hints about what you need to do from the preceding discussion. High scores mean your assertiveness is flagging. If you are involved in exercise, and it isn't helping your "assertiveness quotient," give some thought to how you approach your workouts. Do you engage with a passive attitude? Do you set your goals low and allow them to slip even lower? Do you have self-limiting thoughts about not being able to do any better? If so, challenge yourself! Set more realistic goals. Be tougher with yourself! After all, if you don't like being steamrollered in life, you have to start flexing your muscles—both physically and mentally!

Sometimes when you start a workout, your energy may feel low. As a result, you slip into a desultory routine that leaves you feeling listless when it's over. There's a way to counter this pattern. Begin your workout at a comfortable pace. For example, start off at a moderate walk instead of a shuffling jog. Wake your body up in an easy way that's respectful of your spirit. Forcing yourself into a jog may be too large a transition. After 5 to 10 minutes, increase your pace to a fast walk, but restrain yourself from running. Feel the energy rise inside your body. Get it all warmed up. Soon your spirit will want more. Like a runner on the starting block, your body will yearn for expression. Now, let it go. Let yourself run, and increase your stride to a challenging pace.

There are two key ingredients in this method: respect and intention. Respect comes through accepting yourself as you are in the moment. You may not feel like shoving your chest out and going for it when you begin. If your energy is low, start there. Don't force yourself into a dramatically different pace at the beginning. Intention means that you keep in mind your purpose of becoming more forceful. Sooner or later, your energy will kick in, as long as you remain focused on your goal of improving, of pushing your limits. Sure, there will be days when a fast walk is as much as you are up for. More often, you will come to experience the growing energy inside. You will learn to enjoy the feeling of going flat out. It won't frighten you, and you'll know that the power is all yours.

Jerry felt the world come tumbling down on his 32nd birthday. He had expected that it would have worked out differently, but here he was on a transcontinental flight from L.A. to Boston—another failed relationship, another conversation ending with, "I love you but . . . ." Jerry had a lot of trouble letting people know how he felt. He feared the worst and suppressed all emotion until he literally made himself sick. Then, in a weakened, needy state, he moaned until his partner had had enough of his sniveling. It was just too risky for him to be forthcoming.

Jerry had spent his early 20s in an unusual way. He lived in a yoga ashram with a genuine guru who knew all the answers and preached the doctrine of submission and service. Jerry still practiced yoga every day, but physically he felt quite weak and vulnerable. He looked it, too. He wanted to toughen up, but figured it was too late to join the Marines. So he did the next best thing—he joined a weight-lifting club. He was so intimidated, he quit after the second session. He bought weights for his home, but never used them because he feared the weights would crush him. His luck changed when a cousin moved to town and asked to share lodgings for 6 months. This provided Jerry the critical support he needed. His cousin liked to exercise and began working out with him. What surprised Jerry most was how much anger he began to feel during his workouts. His cousin noticed, too, and after talking it over, Jerry felt more comfortable about grunting and yelling during weight training. He got into it so much that it seemed he was increasing the weights every other week. Jerry's report when he reapplied to the weight club a year later: "I like feeling strong, and weight training helps." It was no coincidence that he felt stronger in other areas of his life as well.

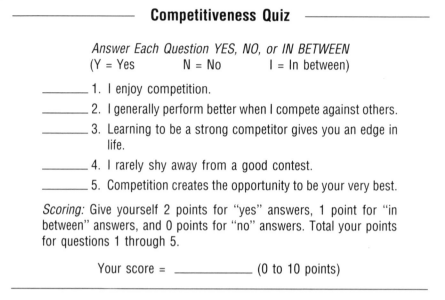

Competitiveness Quiz

Answer Each Question YES, NO, or IN BETWEEN
(Y = Yes   N = No   I = In between)

_____ 1. I enjoy competition.

_____ 2. I generally perform better when I compete against others.

_____ 3. Learning to be a strong competitor gives you an edge in life.

_____ 4. I rarely shy away from a good contest.

_____ 5. Competition creates the opportunity to be your very best.

Scoring: Give yourself 2 points for "yes" answers, 1 point for "in between" answers, and 0 points for "no" answers. Total your points for questions 1 through 5.

Your score = _____ (0 to 10 points)

Where's Your Competitive Spirit?

The world seems to divide neatly into those who like competition and those who don't. Sometimes it gets mislabeled as a "boy-girl" difference, but it has more to do with how you were raised—and what your success rate has been. When you get squashed early in life, your competitive spirit may be dampened. You may end up being a "closet competitor" who is aware of the competitive element in life but rarely lets anyone know she's in the game.

A health club I belong to ran a contest recently. It covered eight events from running to rowing and weight lifting to jumping. It captured most angles of aerobic and anaerobic performance. The contest lasted 12 weeks, during which time you could redo any event to improve your performance for the final tally. Scores were published weekly along with a rank-ordering of competitors. It was a sport psychologist's field day. I was a participant observer in an ongoing field experiment. How would people react? What were the consequences of competition? Who participated? Who didn't? And why?

Each day at the club I would find one group hovering around the weekly postings. The conversation was animated with lots of "I'll get you in that event" challenges. Then there was another group, whispering to each other about how childish the whole thing was and how some people were going to get hurt by pushing too hard just so they can win! It seemed one group was having fun, while the other was being sneering and cynical.

Not that the sneerers didn't have a point. Some of the competitors were definitely getting carried away. Fortunately, there was only one injury—a sprained ankle—but events like the $\dot{V}O_2$max test, a treadmill run until you dropped, could have put some members at risk.

I think everyone was glad when it was over. It had gone on too long, and the pressure of competition hit an overload in the 12th week, when there were no more chances, no more alibis. In the months to come, the spirit of competition lingered, and locker room conversations occasionally reviewed the good old days or the bad old days of the competition, depending on which side of the fence you preferred.

Many competitors said the contest gave them a sense of purpose. It helped direct their workouts. Rather than coming in with an "I wonder what I'll do today" attitude, they knew what they were working toward. People talked about programs of cross-training to enable them to peak at about week 10 of the contest. When one person bettered another's time, it spurred the other to turn the tables. It was a well-rounded contest, and members felt good about overcoming weaknesses and demonstrating strengths.

Curiously, one of the criticisms made in the noncompetitive group was that people were overstressing themselves by coming from highly competitive jobs only to add more competitive pressure in their leisure hours. Few of the competitors complained about this. In fact, those who felt stressed by the competition of their days simply opted out of the contest, saying, "I have enough of this at work." It seemed that people met their needs by either joining in or opting out.

Studies by Robert Helmreich of the University of Texas verify that competition per se isn't bad, but rather the nature of the competitive spirit determines its effects. Helmreich identified people who were mistrustful, secretive, manipulative, and more concerned with winning than with

"SHARPEN YOUR COMPETITIVE EDGE."

performing. This competitive style was found to be detrimental to performance.

Stan Katz and Aimee Liu, authors of *The Success Trap*, also believe you can be too competitive for your own good. They note, "Even in recreation, the push to constantly prove superiority can make you so compulsive about fitness and athletic performance that you increase your risk of injury and deprive yourself of the emotional benefits of exercise."

Interpreting Your Score

Your score on the Competitiveness Quiz reveals your stance toward competition. If you scored 7 or more on the quiz, you thrive on competitive situations, and what better way to cater to this need than by joining in a "friendly" game or a community "fun run." High scorers realize that competition is a way of focusing attention. Your emphasis on competition in sport may be a way of diverting attention from situations that are draining or frustrating. It also takes your mind off problems and gives you something to resolve definitively. Winner or loser, there is always an outcome in a competitive match. It provides a personal yardstick when the rest of life looks like vanilla pudding.

Your best bet in the exercise world comes with activities that offer a competitive challenge. If this is one of your strong motives, you won't do too well on a stationary bicycle or hopping up and down in an aerobics class. Sure, you take your competitive spirit with you no matter where you go, but it's more welcome some places than others.

What if your score is low? Maybe you just don't care to compete, but before saying that, look a little deeper. Maybe your competitive self is hiding. Bring it out carefully. Put yourself in a friendly race, a non-bloodthirsty contest. See how you like it. If it turns you on, great! If not, there are plenty of other ways to find your exercise glue.

Jim was director of finance in a small manufacturing company. He was a whiz with numbers, but felt inept with people. After a painful divorce, he realized he couldn't hide behind his accounting ledgers any more—not if he wanted to get on with life. He complained about the bar scene—"too competitive—the guys are constantly vying with each other to find the best lines, to have the most notches in their belts." He had the same complaint about work, but had been shielded from competition by his irreplaceable talent. Unfortunately, divorce settlements can turn comfortable living standards into marginal conditions. He needed more money, but he felt threatened by the idea of entering a competitive job market.

When Jim was in counseling over his divorce, his therapist detected a hidden competitive side and challenged him to take racquetball lessons. He complied in the interests of mental health. It came as no surprise to his therapist that Jim began to enjoy the dating scene a bit more, that he applied for better jobs, and that he even held out for the best offer. He continued to tell friends he was the noncompetitive type, but they didn't believe him for a minute.

Relationship Quiz

Answer Each Question YES, NO, or IN BETWEEN
(Y = Yes   N = No   I = In between)

_____ 1. I need to be in an intimate relationship to feel okay about myself.

_____ 2. In relationships, I'm preoccupied by my partner's needs and moods.

_____ 3. I usually give more than the other person does in relationships.

_____ 4. I have trouble dealing with feelings of anger or rejection from people close to me.

_____ 5. My self-esteem depends on the way other people feel about me.

Scoring: Give yourself 2 points for "yes" answers, 1 point for "in between" answers, and 0 points for "no" answers. Total your points for questions 1 through 5.

Your score = _____ (0 to 10 points)

Your Intimate Tangles—How Relationships Affect You

Intimate relationships are tricky business. Psychologist Richard Farson, while examining popular myths, came to the conclusion that the opposite of what we believe is often true. For example, we believe that people are very fragile, and we do all kinds of social dances to avoid telling friends what we think of them, because "it would destroy them." Farson said we come closer to the truth when we acknowledge that what is at risk is the relationship, not the individual. He believes people are quite resilient, but relationships are extremely fragile. Statistics are on his side. The percentage of relationships that "die" is far higher than that of people who take their own lives. In fact, our culture has been on a steady growth curve of relationship breakups, as evidenced by high divorce rates, family conflicts, and the casual discarding of long-term personal relationships.

Three types of reactions to relationship traumas have been identified: *disorientation*, *indifference*, and *positive coping*.

Disorientation is a common response that most of us experience in relationship traumas. What distinguishes us is how quickly we pass through this reaction. It may take one person years to get over a failed relationship, while another is working on a new relationship within weeks.

The second kind of reaction, *indifference*, is often a mask. When you have been hurt once too often, it becomes risky to feel. You develop emotional defenses to protect yourself from the impact of loss. You pretend that the relationship didn't mean very much anyway. Call it the "sour grapes" reaction.

Positive coping is a pattern whereby the person goes through a grieving process for the relationship that died, and then gets on with life. The difference between people who react with prolonged disorientation and those who cope positively is that somewhere along the line the positive copers learned how to grieve. Life is about losses—little ones and big ones. It is also about gain, but unless we learn how to let go of the past, we can never move on to make new connections.

This is heady stuff to include in an exercise book. But the fact is that *most people who exercise regularly do so more for psychological reasons than for physical ones*. Once the exercise habit catches on, the rewards come more

"I THOUGHT YOU SAID WE WERE GOING TO EXERCISE *TOGETHER!*"

from how you feel inside than from the pounds you shed or the years added to your lifeline. So, how does exercise connect to this discussion of relationships?

People who have trouble letting go when relationships end or who feel caught in codependent relationships usually suffer from poor self-image. They feel empty unless they are in a relationship, and if the relationship is threatened, they fear personal annihilation. They are like hollow containers who get filled by the other person and who believe they will have nothing left if the relationship ends. All their self-worth is derived from the other. There is precious little they value in themselves.

Exercise has been criticized as a self-centered activity. This may be true, but the evaluation of self-centeredness as bad needs reconsideration. A person who invests too much in others or who depends on others for a sense of well-being needs to become more self-centered. The prescription is to invest in yourself, to fill yourself up, rather than be at the mercy of others' feelings about you.

Is the exercise connection getting any clearer? If you are prone to being in codependent relations, you need to break the habit and develop a new one—with yourself. Exercise is an investment in yourself. It fills you up. It is a statement of "I am important!"--important enough to spend time developing yourself, important enough to value your physical and mental needs, and important enough to put your priorities ahead of anyone else's!

Interpreting Your Score

A low score (3 or less) on the Relationship Quiz suggests you feel pretty self-sufficient and that your identity isn't merged with someone else's. As a low scorer, you will find other motives to help you build an exercise commitment. What if you scored high (7 or more)? Your quiz results indicate your identity is too tied to others and how they feel toward you. Paradoxically, to make your exercise connection, you may need to start exercising in a group activity. A little support at the outset is necessary. It could be in an aerobics class or a walking group. It helps to see others who are taking time for themselves and relishing it. As weeks go by, your activity needs to shift to more self-oriented programs where you can build yourself independently of others. This doesn't mean you have to exercise alone, but rather that the focus is on you in such a way that you know you aren't depending on others to help with your commitment. You might be taking martial arts classes or swimming with a team. It's your performance that counts, though, not the team's or your classmates'.

I like the image of LSD (long, slow, distance) activities in this respect. When you are on a long run or a cycle or even sitting on a rowing machine for 10,000 meters, you have to contend with your own devils. It's a contest of will and self-determination. You can hear the voices telling you to stop or saying this is too hard. Engage those voices. Let them know you can do it. The payoff comes from sticking with yourself. Each day exercising is like going to your personal bank and making a deposit in yourself.

Exercise also has a way of helping you equalize relationships and strengthen the bond. Psychiatrist Bob Hales, coauthor of the *U.S. Army Total Fitness Workout Book*, believes that people in a relationship "can give more, be more empathetic, be more sensitive to their partner's needs, and be more self-actualizing" if they exercise. Also, when people exercise and are in good shape, "sexual issues become less of a problem." Dr. Hales adds that "if the couple runs together, that's intimate time and sexual relations stem from that."

Psychiatrist Ari Kiev, director of the Life Strategy Workshop in New York City, is more philosophical on this point. As a running advocate, Dr. Kiev says running together is great for relationships. "It involves you exposing your vulnerabilities and exploring your limitations, and gives others a chance to support you and the opportunity to bring compassion into a relationship."

There are, of course, predictable mood enhancements from exercise that help to smooth relationship concerns, but unless you understand that you need to invest in yourself, you might develop the aspirin habit of exercise. That is, you overindulge in a bad relationship, get sick, exercise to get better, and then do it all over again. Exercise has to become a valued part of you that by its daily repetition reminds you of your importance to yourself. Choosing activities that work your willpower and provide challenges you can meet is what will make the difference in the long run.

Danny complained about an emptiness in his life. He tried to fill himself through relationships, but his choices often left him bankrupt. He gave and gave until he had nothing left. It was a destructive pattern, but he didn't know how to break it. He looked outside himself for something that only he could provide. He thought others had a magic ingredient that would heal his life and make him feel whole.

In most other respects, he managed well. He had a good job as a systems engineer, some close friends, and hobbies like music and reading. But he felt quite average or, as he put it, "mediocre." He said he had never excelled in anything. He lived in Denver and through a friend's encouragement signed up for an Outward Bound course. It involved technical rock climbing, which at first terrified him. With support and coaching he made it through the 14-day program. He learned he could count on himself—and he liked the feeling. Afterward, Danny joined a rock-climbing club and became quite expert over the years. It gave him a new identity, something he owned and valued. He knew it made a difference, because he didn't feel empty anymore. He even became involved in a long-term relationship that in his own words was "an even give and take."

Personal Power Quiz

Answer Each Question YES, NO, or IN BETWEEN
(Y = Yes   N = No   I = In between)

_____ 1. Mostly I feel like a puppet with someone else pulling my strings.

_____ 2. I have fears about losing control of my life.

_____ 3. It disturbs me when other people make decisions for me.

_____ 4. I am very sensitive to the feeling of being controlled by others.

_____ 5. My job allows me little freedom to make my own decisions.

Scoring: Give yourself 2 points for "yes" answers, 1 point for "in between" answers, and 0 points for "no" answers. Total your points for questions 1 through 5.

Your score = _____ (0 to 10 points)

Personal Power—and the Fear of Being Controlled

I think we all know Henry Kissinger's quote that *"power is the ultimate aphrodisiac."* There has to be great wisdom in it, too, because why else would people be motivated to devote all their energies to careers in politics, business, law, medicine, or a myriad of other professions where a primary payoff is control over others' lives? Feeling power over others is so important that people usurp it in the oddest of roles. Bus drivers who make you wait just so you know who's boss. Secretaries who put you on hold. Clerks who dispense information like bargaining chips. Or children who hold their breath to force a parental concession. Why all this emphasis on power?

David McClelland has studied the need for power over the past 40 years. He sees it as a basic human drive that manifests itself in people from all walks of life. The positive face of power is akin to self-control, being in charge of your life. Negative effects of power come from manipulations of others toward destructive ends. Getting people to do what we want because it's good for us, irrespective of whether it's good for them, becomes a malevolent form of power-tripping—even when things turn out well in the end.

Do we have this need to control others because we feel so little self-control? Or is it a "god complex"? Even when intentions are good, the need to control others is a little like playing Russian roulette. Sooner or later, something goes wrong. This is not to deny the need in society for people to follow rules and be influenced by others. It's just that a compulsive need to control others creates serious problems in relationships.

For most of us, power and control have to do with a feeling of being in charge. We don't want to be a feather in the windstorm of life. If we have been buffeted about too much, we may develop countertendencies to resist all efforts to control us. We may also try to dominate others in the vein of "the best defense is a good offense."

As children, we may have been overcontrolled by domineering parents and not allowed to develop a sense of personal power. The biography of Adolf Hitler provides a tragic example of this scenario. Less extreme cases also have damaging effects on our egos. To rectify the situation, we may turn the situation around when we grow older—but in these instances, we miss the essential point. As Victor Frankl, psychiatrist and author of *Man's Search for Meaning*, theorized, the highest sense of control we can have is over our own lives and, at the deepest level, over our own thoughts and feelings.

According to social psychologists John French and Bertram Raven, power is something you give to others because you want something in return. It's an exchange. You may want to earn a livelihood, and therefore allow a boss to tell you what to do. Or you may want someone to like you, and do her bidding to receive her attention. In the extreme you may want to survive and, therefore, comply with orders. In a free society, many people believe they can opt out of the control matrix, but this is a myth. As long as you have needs, you are subject to being controlled.

It's sensible to want to be in charge of your life. It's also important to acknowledge that manipulation is not a dirty word. In a social world, everything can be seen as a manipulation. I interact with others to get my needs met. They do the same. We are constantly trying to influence and manipulate each other. If I doubt my ability to say no to your influence attempts, I may either withdraw or try to control you. If I am uncertain of my own influencing skills, I may be sneaky and indirect or I may become aggressively demanding.

Interpreting Your Score

If you score high (7 or more) on the Personal Power Quiz, you feel worried about how much control you exert over your life. You may be overly sensitive when control issues rise up in relationships. In fact, you may see them when they're not there. What you are really concerned about is whether you can control yourself.

The fitness connection is aptly described by Lesley Howes, owner of the Crosby Street Studio in New York City: "In a world where nothing is predictable, exercise becomes something a person can count on." But it's more than that. It's also the sense of gaining control over your body through exercise that makes you feel more in charge of your life. And when people exercise enough to experience their physical strength, they interpret this newfound sense of power as psychological as much as physical, according to Michael O'Shea, director of the Sports Training Institute in New York City.

If your score is high, you might not do well in structured activities where there's a teacher-student relationship, especially if you come under intense scrutiny. You need to work on finding your own control center. Activities where you can go at your own pace, where you get to choose how much, how fast, and when to exercise will reinforce the sense of your being in charge.

Make yourself the expert. Learn as much as you can about your sport. If you choose an activity like weight training, take a few lessons from an expert. Get a bibliography so you can understand the principles of training and how to work different muscles. Ask people in the weight room what works best for them. By learning how to develop your body the way you want it to be, you will experience a growing sense of mastery. Through practice and commitment, this sphere of personal power will spread to other areas of your life as well.

High scorers might also want to consider an activity that, on the surface, appears to be the opposite of what you need. Martial arts training develops self-control, but only through a process of giving up all control to another, the sensai. It seems paradoxical, but it works. I relate it to a similar phenomenon in the field of psychotherapy. In working toward self-reliance, psychotherapy clients must often pass through a period of extreme dependency on the therapist. It is only in working through this dependency, by allowing themselves to fully experience it in a healthy, therapeutic environment, that clients get beyond it. I suppose the risk in martial arts training is the same as that in therapy—the outcome of this "independence training" may be contingent on the qualities of the person doing the coaching. It's not guaranteed, but some careful shopping around can increase the chances for success.

Remember that the goal is to transfer your worries about external control by others to the creation of an internal feeling of self-control. Make it a personal meditation, that is, what you focus on while you are exercising. Develop self-control through your exercise commitment. What better way to see results than through a fitness program that produces both performance and body changes.

As a low scorer (3 or less), you may have discovered some of these exercise connections on your own. If not, keep them in mind. Your sense of personal power may need reinforcement from time to time and it's good to know just how to get it.

Gary had a black belt in tae kwon do and worked as an instructor in his spare time. He seemed so unlike what you might expect—easygoing and not particularly athletic. Yet he was good enough not only to earn a black belt, but also to win a few prestigious competitions. Gary came from a tough area of the city. His father had bullied him into fighting back whenever he got hassled, but Gary usually ended up the loser. As he grew older, he got threatened more easily and usually overreacted. A shrug of the shoulders might have been more beneficial than a boxing posture. After too many losses, he joined a karate club and worked his way up the ladder. What he began to internalize, however, wasn't a killer instinct, but a feeling of self-control, an inner calm amidst external storms. Although he continued to live in the same neighborhood, his fights gradually decreased. It wasn't that he didn't get challenged, it was just that he didn't need to react. He simply didn't threaten easily.

Reviewing Your Social Motives

There is much to digest in trying to understand your social needs and how they connect to an exercise program. An error we frequently make in trying to develop ourselves is being too literal about how we go about changing. An example can be seen in the person who decides to conquer anxiety by telling himself not to be anxious. It just makes matters worse. Another error is in not recognizing how much our psychology is based in our bodies. When we change our bodies, we invariably affect our minds. Sometimes this occurs through what we do. An example would be making ourselves stay on a treadmill at a tough pace for 30 minutes a day, 5 days a week. It teaches us something about self-control. Other times it happens through how we do it—for example, when we focus in weight training on our power to overcome obstacles, rather than concentrate on feelings of weakness.

Perhaps it reduces to a body-mind metaphor for aspects of our life. If we can use exercise as a source of creative energy for reshaping our bodies, why can't we turn it into a place where we work on what we need in our social lives. Our interpersonal needs can then serve as guides to action.

Completing Your Profile

A graph is provided in Figure 5.1 so you can create a visual overview of your scores. This is similar to previous ones in chapters 3 and 4. Write your six social motive scores in the spaces provided on the graph. On the left side of the graph, you will find a scale ranging from 0 to 10. Start with your score on the Sociability Quiz. Draw a line corresponding to your score (0 to 10) across the top of the Sociability column. Then shade in the area in the column beneath the line. Do the same for the other motives.

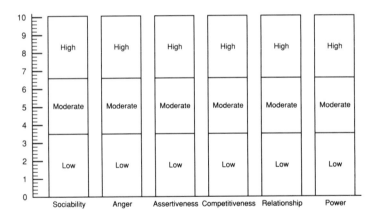

Figure 5.1 In the graph above, each column represents one of the six social motives. For each, draw a line corresponding to your score across the column, then shade in the area below your line.

The Social Motives Profile you have just created will help you compare your six scores. You can determine which is your highest and lowest. If your social motives are uniformly high, this calls your attention to the potency of these motives for supporting your exercise habit. Conversely, if they are uniformly low, it means you may have to look to other motives to reinforce an exercise program.

Take a few minutes to consider what this graph says about you. Question yourself about any reactions to this profile. Does it make sense to you? Does it accurately portray who you are? Do you feel good about it? Make notes on your reactions so you have a record of any things you might want to emphasize or change as you go about designing an exercise program in the next section of this book.

CHAPTER 6

WEIGHING YOUR NEEDS, TRIMMING YOUR OPTIONS

"When I have to choose between two evils, I always try to pick the one I haven't tried yet."
MAE WEST

The Natural Choice

I was talking with an old friend the other day. He had just returned from an overseas assignment and was complaining about having gained 25 pounds. It wasn't the first time this had happened. He also mentioned that he had suffered from high blood pressure 10 years ago and needed to remain watchful on that front. He told me he was going to start exercising again. I nodded "Uh huh" and waited for his explanation. John didn't know much about my sport theory, and I didn't want to lead him to conclusions about the "right" exercise choice.

What followed was a self-analysis that went something like this:

"I'm not a very sociable guy—that's why team sports never appealed to me. I don't like having to depend on others. Besides, I prefer being on my own. I discovered running years ago, and it stuck for a long time. I like it—it's efficient exercise. It makes the best use of my time. I can just tie on my shoes, get in about 3 miles, shower, and be ready for work. The whole thing is only 30 minutes out of my day. Another reason I don't like team sports is the competitive bit—I hate competing. Running is something I do at my own pace. I rarely run with anyone else. And my doctor thinks it's good for me, especially now that I have these extra pounds to lose."

From the Fitness Incentives Quizzes we reviewed, we can see that John hit on four motives that were important to him: sociability, competitiveness, health concerns, and weight worry. John wasn't looking for meaning in his life, nor was his self-esteem a concern. He had a healthy degree of vanity but wasn't obsessed with how he looked. What he didn't mention was that his high blood pressure was related to feelings of anxiety he experienced at work. Nor did he mention his marriage to a woman he described as "domineering." In another conversation, John talked about the outlet running gave him from feelings of being smothered by his wife. He had a chance to be alone and sort things out for himself. Then he could return home with his own opinions in clearer perspective. This means we can add two other motives to his list: moods and tension, and relationship problems.

There was one more. John earned his doctorate at age 26 and had pursued a demanding career over the past 15 years. He was an achiever, and although he didn't compete in road races, he had invested in a few gadgets that measured the time and distance of his runs, which he religiously recorded in a special training log. So now we are talking about achievement.

All together, it was a complex brew. John had figured it out over the years, but his initial contacts with fitness and sport were trial and error. Sometimes he did what he thought he should do, other times he did what his friends were into at the time. Eventually he came to choose something that met his needs, not someone else's or the dictates of a current fitness fad. Running worked for him—and had circumstances been different or had he taken the time to make a more complete survey, other sports might have worked as well.

John's decision seemed self-evident—a natural choice. In hindsight, it didn't seem to require much effort to decide that running was his thing. What the story doesn't reveal are the trips John took down dead-end trails or the times he lost sight of his needs and, as a consequence, couldn't see his toes when he stood up.

Knowing What It's All About

Living in a culture that idolizes health, beauty, longevity, sexuality, and lots of smooth, well-muscled skin, how is it that fitness regulars constitute only 10% of the adult population? What makes it such a struggle for people like John to keep on top of their needs?

Maybe we're mad at life's unfairness. Some people seem to have it so easy. They are born with bodies that require little maintenance to look great. Most of us have to work at it. Or maybe our minds haven't quite caught up with all the evolutionary leaps the world has been making. The problem is, by the time we figure out the changes that took us from the farms and back-breaking chores to sedentary jobs in offices and high-tech John Deere tractors, the fat cells may have migrated to our ankles.

I think most 20th-century-ites are still coming to terms with the fact that the body beautiful doesn't happen by itself or that sitting at a desk doesn't constitute work at a body level.

What may feed the delusion is a growing confidence that modern medicine and science will come to the rescue. I have a neighbor who bought a treadmill so she could "think exercise." She was 5-foot-6 and 195 pounds, with the most singular kind of willpower I have ever known. On her 35th birthday, in December, she made up her mind to fit into a size 8 by summer. She also decided to go from an AA cup to a C. And how was she going to do all this? For Amy, it was a two-step process. First, she starved herself for 6 months and dropped down to 120 pounds. She then scheduled in a little cosmetic surgery—liposuction for the hips, and implants for the breasts. Voila! She never even had to turn on the treadmill (although she did say it kept her on her diet by symbolizing the torture she would otherwise have to endure).

Personally, I have strong reservations about Amy's self-change strategy. I can't ignore medical evidence of the dangers of her surgical procedures. More centrally, I wonder what lessons about life she learned through this "quick fix." What will she do next time she doesn't like something about herself or her life? And what if there are no "easy" solutions? I can understand her motivation. It makes me feel bad, nonetheless, that she was socialized to see treadmills (and other forms of exercise) as torture. Her lifelong allies are more likely to come from self-sustained health care programs like exercise than from instant beauty traps like surgery and yo-yo diets.

This is not to say that fitness is all about the body and physical looks. The motivational profiles you created in earlier chapters don't rely on body image alone. There are psychological, social, and less aesthetically oriented, physical motives. Finding out how your motives relate to fitness is what we need to work on now. You have collected a good deal of information about your motives in the previous chapters, but you may be having problems sorting through all the interpretations of what you should do.

Before you can learn about the possibilities of exercise, you have to clear your mind of preconceptions. Some of your biases come through attitudes you pick up from others about exercise, and the media are also a major influence on your beliefs.

Understanding Your Mind-Set

Like my immigrant parents who had no time for exercise, many people are critical of fitness regulars. Even though it takes real dedication to stick to an exercise program, some critics label exercise as little more than a selfish preoccupation. You can be excessive in exercise as in any other sphere of life, but what the critics miss is how much exercise plays into character development. What they also fail to realize is that it isn't a matter for debate any longer. Argue all you like, the fact is that our bodies *need* exercise. Sure, you can get exercise by raking the lawn as much as from jogging around the block. But if you don't have a lawn, and you sit at a desk all day, and you drive to and from work, then what?

The Transitional Generation

Imagine growing up in a family that regularly attends fitness classes together or that has an exercise room for everyone's use. Picture a family where the parents bustle around the kitchen making breakfast after their morning run. What kinds of messages do these images convey about fitness?

If you're over 30, you may have grown up with very different messages about exercise. You belong to the transitional generation. Fitness wasn't part of the culture of the fifties and sixties. You weren't bombarded with fitness facts every time you opened a newspaper. Notions of health weren't so nakedly and muscularly portrayed. It's only recently that health clubs began to outnumber pool halls and bowling alleys. Whatever you needed to know about fitness, you had to decipher on your own. At least in terms of values and media information, future generations are likely to be far more aware of the role of exercise in a healthy lifestyle.

You may have been raised in a time when women weren't supposed to exercise and men were only supposed to do it at the company picnic or for 5 minutes when they jumped out of bed in the morning. It may be hard changing your lifestyle to suit this modern-day emphasis on fitness. You need information that comes from inside you. You need to be able to identify your lifelong motives and understand how to channel them into an exercise habit. That's what you are in the process of doing now.

Media Misinformation

In addition to overcoming all the messages from childhood, you also have to deal with misinformation from the media. Magazine columnists and writers may have their hearts in the right place, but in their desire to entice you to exercise, they often oversell the product.

It's not just that media presentations are wrapped around sexy, young bodies, but that somehow it always looks easy. In your gut, you know it's not—or if you don't, you discover the truth the hard way. I'm not simply referring to the physical side. If we go about exercise carefully, I think that part can be managed so as to avoid pain and injury. More centrally, I'm concerned with the emotional agenda—all the ways you have to confront yourself and own up to who you are and what your body can *and* can't do.

Most fitness campaigns have a disturbing quality of disregarding the mind that sits atop the exercising body. A 1990 TV documentary on exercise typified this approach. The program interspersed expert opinions about medical benefits of exercise with staged footage of people smiling as they ran or sat on stationary bicycles. There were the usual cautionary notes about beginning slowly, setting reasonable objectives, and seeking medical consultation when indicated. When it came time for the experts to tell us what exercise programs were best, advice was limited to physiological considerations like whether the activity used large muscle groups, included repetitive motions, was oxygen-fueled, lasted for so many minutes, and so forth. Examples of running, swimming, and cycling were used as illustrations. The documentary was virtually devoid of information about the psychology of exercise, other than saying that it makes you "feel good."

Another way we get misinformation is through media ads for fitness products. The slant is minimally informative and usually prejudicial. If anything, the ads may cause potential jocks to feel guilty and retreat even further. You may remember the Nautilus campaign that proclaimed "Fitness is everything" alongside pictures of magnificently muscled bodies. What was the message? A beautiful body is everything? And what if you don't have one and believe you are in such bad shape that you can never get one?

Or what about Nike's listing of health approaches from psychoanalysis to numerology, followed by a photo of a hard-bodied runner with the caption "Just do it." This is great! A prescription for acting without thinking.

It seems reasonable to ask the question, if "fitness is everything" and you should "just do it," where do you start? You might think you should be doing whatever is being pictured in the ads and that, that way, you will end up looking just like those picture-perfect athletes. Fortunately, most of us realize sooner or later that it's not so easy or that it's downright impossible. But then we are left with the question, what do we do? My response is to look within and discover what you need and what you can get from the fitness world. This requires more than a little thought.

Know Thyself—First!

It's true we can spend too much time analyzing and not enough time doing. The difficulty comes when in our impulsiveness to get going, we

"I WONDER WHICH SUITS ME BEST?"

"leap to confusion." If you are planning a lifelong change in habits, you need to take time and give yourself all the attention you deserve.

Consider an analogy. A young woman wants to know what career to pursue. She visits a guidance counselor who tests her aptitudes and interests with sophisticated psychological tests. The profiles derived from the tests guide her career choices. She now knows what the options are and how suited she is to success in different fields.

So what's the parallel for the novice exerciser? It can't be to just do it! That's great advice after you have figured out exactly what it is you need to be doing—and, perhaps more importantly, *why* you should do it in the first place. So let's put all of this into a very personal perspective of why you are going to exercise.

Before the What Is the Why

Before you get to the *what* question, you have to know your answers to the question *why*. Why are you doing it? Looking over your Fitness Incentives Quizzes in chapters 3, 4, and 5 will help you answer this question.

Part 1. Analyzing Your High Scores

What were your highest scores? Did you have two or more scores tied for first place? Let's take it a step at a time and organize your answers.

Step 1.   Review your scores for the Body, Psychological, and Social Motive Profiles (Figures 3.1, 4.1, and 5.1). In the section below, you will be asked to analyze your top 3 motives out of the 18 that you evaluated.

How do you know which are the top 3? You may have tie scores for a number of motives. List below all the scores—up to a maximum of seven—that you consider to be high scores for you. Write in the name of the motive and the score you received on the quiz. Leave the space under the word "rank" empty for now.

High Score Motives	Score	Rank
_____	____	____
_____	____	____
_____	____	____
_____	____	____
_____	____	____
_____	____	____
_____	____	____

Now, think about each one and evaluate its relative importance. It may be that two motives are close, for example, health concerns and a quest for youth, but one feels more important to you than the other—even though they may show the same score. It may be that you have high scores on personal power and competitiveness, but the central concern for you is being in charge of your life. In this case, personal power would be a more compelling motive than competitiveness.

When you have evaluated and compared scores on your highest fitness incentives, rank-order them from top to bottom, assigning a rank of #1 to the most important and so on down the list until you have given the lowest number (#7 if you listed 7 motives) to the one that is least motivating in this group.

Step 2.   For each of your top 3 motives (Ranks #1, #2, and #3), fill in a Motive Analysis Box (Figures 6.2, 6.3, and 6.4), as illustrated in Figure 6.1. You are asked to answer a series of questions:

1. **What is the motive?**

   Write in the name of the motive (e.g., self-esteem).

2. **What does your score mean?**

   In your own words, write down what your score on this motive means to you, that is, how you interpret your high score. Also, indicate how comfortable you are with your score. You may like the fact that you score high, or you may want to change it. A good example is the self-esteem score, where high numbers indicate significant dissatisfaction with yourself. If this score is high for you, you probably would want to see it change—and you should be well motivated to make this happen.

3. **How does exercise relate to this motive?**

   From what you have read in chapters 3, 4, and 5, and from your personal feelings about exercise, how would an exercise program address this motive? What would exercise do for you that would satisfy this need? You may want to refer to Table 6.1 as a guide in responding. This table provides ideas about the underlying concerns in each of the motives.

   Answer this question without specifying a particular type of exercise program. This is a general question, so respond in a more comprehensive manner regarding the benefits of exercise to this motivational source.

4. **What specific exercise plans would be best suited to this motive?**

   Now you can be specific. Indicate which exercise programs might be best for this motive. Refer again to Table 6.1 to help you identify exercise programs most suited to your needs. List fitness programs or sports that you are *attracted* to and that you feel *capable* of performing.

5. **Which exercise plan or sport, if any, are you avoiding?**

   Of the options available to you, are there any exercise programs or sports you are avoiding, even though they may be beneficial? If so, write them down with a comment indicating what would have to change for you to participate.

   Don't include activities that are physically impossible for you to do or that are impractical (e.g., surfing, if you live in Alaska!). Identifying activities you are avoiding may give you clues about future avenues to personal growth.

6. **Which exercise plan or sport is most attractive all-around?**

   Select the *one* exercise program or sport that makes most sense to you in terms of (a) satisfying this motive and (b) fitting into your life at this time.

Repeat the analysis two more times: There are three Motive Analysis Boxes (Figures 6.2, 6.3, and 6.4), one for each of your top 3 motives. Repeat the analysis, answering all the questions for each motive. Think about each motive independently from the others. That is, don't answer with the same sport or exercise plans just because you want to be consistent.

Step 3.   After completing the three analyses, write down the sport or exercise program that you listed as your answer to question 6 in each Motive Analysis Box. It may be the same answer in all three cases, but if not, rank-order your answers (1st, 2nd, and 3rd) from your "most preferred" to your "least preferred" activity.

Best Exercise Program or Sport for Highest 3 Motives

1st: _____

2nd: _____

3rd: _____

Now turn the page to begin analyzing your high scores.

MOTIVE ANALYSIS—HIGH SCORES

High motive: Rank #1

1. What is the motive?

Relationships

2. What does your score mean?

I feel very dependent on others for how I feel about myself. When I'm in a relationship, I seem to defer to my partner's needs all the time. It's not fair to my partner, either, because I neglect myself and complain in subtle ways that I'm not getting what I need. I guess I blame my partner when I'm really the one who disempowers myself.

3. How does exercise relate to this motive?

I think if I exercised, I would feel better about myself. I would be doing something for me—taking responsibility for my life! I would probably even look better, which would make me feel better about myself. I think I would feel less needy, less dependent, and more capable of being in a good, give-and-take relationship—or being alone if I choose to be.

4. What specific exercise plans would be best suited to this motive?

I think I could get into jogging. I like the outdoors, and I could start at my own pace. It might be difficult to get going in the beginning, so I might join a running club for the first few months.

5. Which exercise plan or sport, if any, are you avoiding?

I feel intimidated by the idea of weight training. I don't have a very positive body image, and I feel weak a lot of the time. But something inside tells me it would be good for me to flex my muscles.

6. Which exercise plan or sport is most attractive all-around?

Jogging is my best bet. I know it's good to balance jogging with some light weight work. That'll be a way of easing myself into body building.

Figure 6.1   A sample Motive Analysis Box.

MOTIVE ANALYSIS—HIGH SCORES

<u>High motive: Rank #1</u>

1. What is the motive?

2. What does your score mean?

3. How does exercise relate to this motive?

4. What specific exercise plans would be best suited to this motive?

5. Which exercise plan or sport, if any, are you avoiding?

6. Which exercise plan or sport is most attractive all-around?

Figure 6.2   Analyzing your rank #1 high score.

MOTIVE ANALYSIS—HIGH SCORES

<u>High motive: Rank #2</u>

1. What is the motive?

2. What does your score mean?

3. How does exercise relate to this motive?

4. What specific exercise plans would be best suited to this motive?

5. Which exercise plan or sport, if any, are you avoiding?

6. Which exercise plan or sport is most attractive all-around?

Figure 6.3 Analyzing your rank #2 high score.

MOTIVE ANALYSIS—HIGH SCORES

High motive: Rank #3

1. What is the motive?

2. What does your score mean?

3. How does exercise relate to this motive?

4. What specific exercise plans would be best suited to this motive?

5. Which exercise plan or sport, if any, are you avoiding?

6. Which exercise plan or sport is most attractive all-around?

Figure 6.4 Analyzing your rank #3 high score.

Table 6.1 Using Your Motives to Guide Your Choices

How to Use This Table

Name of the motive

Focus:	Key that connects the motive to exercise
Look for:	Tells what you want to achieve
Best bets:	Describes qualities to look for in an activity
Examples:	Offers concrete suggestions that *may* apply
Poor bets:	Identifies qualities to avoid in an activity
Examples:	Offers concrete suggestions that *may* apply

THE BODY MOTIVES

Vanity

Focus:	Improving my looks and how I feel about them
Look for:	Enhancement of physical self/body dimensions
Best bets:	Activities that emphasize alignment and body definition
Examples:	Body shaping, targeted calisthenics, weight training, circuit training
Poor bets:	Activities that neglect body areas or alignment
Examples:	Jogging, cycling, golf, stair climbing, leisure walking

---

Sexuality

Focus:	Enjoying my sensual self and promoting sexual feelings
Look for:	Getting out of your mind and into your body
Best bets:	Activities that emphasize body awareness and expression
Examples:	Yoga, modern dance, ballroom dance, synchronized swimming, belly dancing
Poor bets:	Activities that bind the body or require emotional suppression
Examples:	Body building, hard contact sports (e.g., football), treadmill running

Addictive behaviors

Focus:	Avoiding negative addictions, developing positive habits
Look for:	Reliable participation with friendly standards
Best bets:	A defined, well-rounded, injury prevention program
Examples:	Cross-training plus yoga, low-impact aerobics, running plus swimming, hiking
Poor bets:	Activities that promote perfectionism, compulsivity, or tendency to injury
Examples:	Running without cross-training, highly competitive team or racquet sports

Weight worry

Focus:	Losing weight and/or maintaining a desirable weight
Look for:	Consistency, continuity, and caloric consumption
Best bets:	Moderate- to high-intensity activities of long duration
Examples:	Jogging, aerobics, speed walking, stair climbing, cycling, circuit training, rowing, pool running
Poor bets:	Short-spurt, anaerobic, or low-intensity/short-duration activities
Examples:	Easy swimming, body building, yoga, volleyball

Health worry

Focus:	Doing my best to stay healthy
Look for:	Moderate and regular aerobic conditioning
Best bets:	Medically sanctioned moderate, nonstressful aerobic workouts
Examples:	Low-impact aerobics, swimming, jogging, cycling, walking
Poor bets:	Anaerobic, highly competitive, risk-oriented activities
Examples:	Body building, sky diving, racquet sports, contact sports

Quest for youth

Focus:	Feeling young and maintaining my vitality
Look for:	Strength, flexibility, and aerobic conditioning
Best bets:	Activities that use the whole body and stress flexibility
Examples:	Swimming, yoga, body shaping, low-impact aerobics, cross-training, cross-country skiing
Poor bets:	Activities that work limited body areas and decrease flexibility
Examples:	Bowling, running, cycling

(Cont.)

Table 6.1 (Continued)

THE PSYCHOLOGICAL MOTIVES

Self-esteem

Focus:	Wanting to feel better about myself
Look for:	Realistic and achievable goals
Best bets:	Activities where you set the standards—and *just show up*
Examples:	Exercise walking, time-limited running, swimming, stationary cycling, rowing, aerobics classes
Poor bets:	Activities with built-in performance standards or comparisons.
Examples:	Ballet, racquet sports, golf

Achievement

Focus:	Setting worthwhile goals and achieving them
Look for:	A personal challenge
Best bets:	Challenging activities with clear and measurable outcomes
Examples:	Track events, golf, rock climbing, weight training, lap swimming, alpine skiing, curling
Poor bets:	Activities where standards are vague or performance is unevaluated.
Examples	Aerobics, routine calisthenics, jogging, leisure swimming

Moods and tension

Focus:	Controlling my moods and easing my tension
Look for:	Releasing tension and stimulating positive feelings
Best bets:	Continuous-movement, aerobic, oxygen-fueled activities
Examples:	Aerobics, running, swimming, speed walking, t'ai chi, yoga
Poor bets:	Anaerobic activities, ones that permit mental worry or that resemble life's stress.
Examples:	Racquet sports, highly competitive team sports, body building

Stress

Focus:	Reducing my stress level—feeling more at ease
Look for:	Taking "time out" and creating body/mind release
Best bets:	Regular, aerobic activities that distract or control the mind
Examples:	Yoga, running, t'ai chi, circuit training, aerobic dance, synchronized swimming, skating
Poor bets:	Anaerobic activities, ones that permit mental worry or that resemble life's stress..
Examples:	Racquet sports, highly competitive team sports, body building

Search for meaning

Focus:	Experiencing a sense of purpose and meaning in my life
Look for:	Opportunity for intensive inner journey
Best bets:	Activities that are rhythmical, repetitive, and inner-directed
Examples:	T'ai chi, yoga, long-distance running, cycling, swimming, mountaineering, canoeing
Poor bets:	Activities that are other-directed or performance-oriented
Examples:	Aerobics, racquet sports, golf, body building

Playfulness

Focus:	Having fun and encouraging my playful spirit
Look for:	Non-goal-oriented, expressive, and spontaneous movements
Best bets:	Activities that are gamelike or that encourage self-expression
Examples:	"Friendly" volleyball and team sports, skating, frisbee, "new (noncompetitive) games"
Poor bets:	Repetitive, rule-bound, or performance-oriented activities.
Examples:	Stationary cycling, running on a treadmill

(Cont.)

Table 6.1 (Continued)

THE SOCIAL MOTIVES

Sociability

Focus:	Enjoying being with people
Look for:	Verbal and nonverbal interaction possibilities
Best bets:	Activities where you engage with others and feel their support
Examples:	Folk dancing, walking/hiking clubs, ''new (noncompetitive) games,'' bowling, fishing, camping
Poor bets:	Activities where interaction is restricted
Examples:	Swimming, solitary running, cycling

Anger control

Focus:	Controlling my anger and releasing the pressure
Look for:	Performance-free, safe, physical catharsis
Best bets:	Noncompetitive, aerobic, repetitive-movement activities
Examples:	Running, cycling, swimming, aerobics, martial arts
Poor bets:	Competitive, performance-oriented, anaerobic activities
Examples:	Body building, racquet sports, bowling

Assertiveness

Focus:	Taking care of my needs, asserting myself when necessary
Look for:	Holding my ground, feeling my strength
Best bets:	Activities that develop your strength, expressiveness, and grounding
Examples:	Power lifting, aikido, jazz ballet, windsurfing
Poor bets:	Activities that increase introspection or ignore grounding
Examples:	Swimming, cycling, easy jogging

Competitiveness

Focus:	Enjoying the challenge of competition and the thrill of winning
Look for:	Competing for enjoyment
Best bets:	Competitive activities that offer a fair challenge
Examples:	All competitive games and sports
Poor Bets:	Goalless, noncompetitive activities
Examples:	Aerobics, yoga, hiking, walking

Relationships

Focus:	Valuing myself in or out of relationship
Look for:	Keeping the ''I'' in exercise
Best bets:	Activities that ground you and develop your sense of self
Examples:	Fencing, Aikido, windsurfing, alpine skiing, goal-oriented endurance activities
Poor bets:	Amorphous, unrewarding activities or ones where you get submerged in the group
Examples:	Aerobics, goalless walking or running, team sports

Personal power

Focus:	Feeling in control of my destiny, being in charge
Look for:	Getting grounded in your own reality
Best bets:	Self-directed activities where progress is self-assessed
Examples:	T'ai chi, running, kayaking, rock climbing, weight training, windsurfing
Poor bets:	Other-directed activities or ones where comparisons are fostered
Examples:	Racquet sports, golf, team sports

Part 2. Analyzing Your Low Scores

It's not just high scores that have significance. Perhaps the clearest example is the sociability motive, where a high score indicates a preference for being with people, but a low score is equally significant and may suggest either a need to be alone or a social anxiety that you would like to overcome.

Step 1.   To complete your self-analysis, review your scores on the body, psychological, and social motives, and choose three low scores that concern you. You may have been surprised by some of your scores, or you may have thought they should be higher. In either case, write the names of these motives in the spaces below.

Three Low Scores That Concern Me Are . . .

1st: _____

2nd: _____

3rd: _____

Step 2.   Now that these are identified, use the Motive Analysis Boxes provided in Figures 6.5, 6.6, and 6.7 to dissect what these motives imply for your exercise plan. Answer each of the following questions:

1. **What is the motive?**

    Write in the name of the motive (e.g., competitiveness).

2. **What does your score mean?**

    In your own words, write down what your score on this motive means to you, that is, how you interpret your low score. Indicate what makes you uncomfortable with this score. You may think, for example, that you should be more competitive or that your avoidance of competition reflects a deeper fear of personal rejection.

3. **How does exercise relate to this motive?**

    From what you have read and from your appreciation of exercise, how would an exercise program be designed to satisfy this motive? For example, you may want to avoid competition and, therefore, stay away from any activity where your performance can be compared with someone else's. Remember, this is a general question, so give your personal impressions of the relevance of exercise to this motive. You may want to refer to information in Table 6.1.

4. **What specific exercise plans would be best suited to this motive?**

   Now you can be specific. Indicate which exercise programs might be best for dealing with your low score on this motive. The sport or exercise programs would be the "poor bets" listed in Table 6.1.

5. **Which exercise plan or sport, if any, are you avoiding?**

   Of the options available to you, are there any exercise programs or sports you are avoiding, even though they might prove beneficial? This question is particularly relevant to low scores. Try to identify activities that might prove helpful to your personal development, even though they may run counter to the need expressed by this low score.

6. **Which exercise plan or sport is most attractive all-around?**

   Select the one exercise program or sport that makes most sense to you in terms of (a) satisfying this motive and (b) fitting into your life at this time.

Step 3.   List the activities you came up with in answering question 6 of each of the three Motive Analysis Boxes. If you came up with more than one activity, rank order them 1st, 2nd, and 3rd.

Best Exercise Program or Sport for Low Motives

1st: _____

2nd: _____

3rd: _____

Now turn the page to begin analyzing your low scores.

MOTIVE ANALYSIS—LOW SCORES

Low motive: Rank #1

1. What is the motive?

2. What does your score mean?

3. How does exercise relate to this motive?

4. What specific exercise plans would be best suited to this motive?

5. Which exercise plan or sport, if any, are you avoiding?

6. Which exercise plan or sport is most attractive all-around?

Figure 6.5 Analyzing your rank #1 low score.

MOTIVE ANALYSIS—LOW SCORES

Low motive: Rank #2

1. What is the motive?

2. What does your score mean?

3. How does exercise relate to this motive?

4. What specific exercise plans would be best suited to this motive?

5. Which exercise plan or sport, if any, are you avoiding?

6. Which exercise plan or sport is most attractive all-around?

Figure 6.6   Analyzing your rank #2 low score.

MOTIVE ANALYSIS—LOW SCORES

Low motive: Rank #3

1. What is the motive?

2. What does your score mean?

3. How does exercise relate to this motive?

4. What specific exercise plans would be best suited to this motive?

5. Which exercise plan or sport, if any, are you avoiding?

6. Which exercise plan or sport is most attractive all-around?

Figure 6.7   Analyzing your rank #3 low score.

Part 3. Comparing Results from High and Low Scores

The next part of the analysis is to compare your answers from high and low scores. What activities did you uncover? And how did they meet your needs? If you were thorough in your self-appraisal, you might have come up with two kinds of answers. You might have discovered an activity or two that suit your needs right now. This would be an activity you would feel inclined to do with relatively little resistance. It would readily fit your lifestyle and satisfy your needs. You might have also identified activities for the future.

Let's deal with the present first. All you need to do here is list your choice. We will look at some of the more practical considerations in the final chapter. If you have two or three activities that emerged from your analysis, list your other choices as alternatives.

My Exercise Choice

First choice _____

_____

(Alternatives) _____

_____

_____

Part 4. Listing Future Possibilities

You may also have discovered an activity that outstrips your current state of readiness to engage the exercise world, but one that appeals to you nonetheless. This activity should be noted here for future reference. It may become more relevant to your needs as time goes on. For the moment, just make note of it.

A possible activity for the future is _____

_____

_____

P·A·R·T · III

HOLDING ON TO THE EXERCISE HABIT

CHAPTER 7

GETTING STARTED

"Looking back, my life seems like one long obstacle race,
with me as its chief obstacle."
JACK PAAR

Are You Ready?

What have you accomplished so far? You have identified your exercise motives and learned how they direct you toward specific exercise programs. This is critical to your success. Starting out on the right path will make your journey toward developing the exercise habit much easier.

Knowing the right exercise program for your needs means you can begin making plans. You might have to do some research on where to go, what to buy, or whom to see. There are technical details of how much exercise you should do in the beginning, specific settings for weights in a body-building program, or warm-up routines that will keep you injury-free. It's important to become familiar with the physical side of your program—exercise physiology. You don't have to become an expert, but it's good to find out about your resting heart rate, blood pressure, and body composition (or how much extra fat you are carrying around). You might also want to know how many calories you will burn in your exercise program, how fast your heart should be beating, and what precautions you should take when exercising in hot or cold climates. Checking with your doctor or going for a physical evaluation at a fitness center is a good way to start your data-gathering process.

This book isn't about exercise physiology, though. It's about the most neglected dimension of exercise participation—your psychological side, the missing link that connects you to exercise. What most people skip in their program planning is understanding the psychological side. You need to prepare your mind as well as your body for regular exercise. We don't think about getting certain equipment for our minds when we start exercising, although we may spend hours researching the right shoes. Yet we do have to equip our minds. With what? Information about what the path may be like as you shift from a sedentary lifestyle to an active one. That's where we're going now. We're going to preview the path to developing the exercise habit.

Why Start? Why Stop?

Maybe you've been there before—starting an exercise program and then dropping out? If so, you're like a lot of other people. In fact, 50% of people who begin an exercise program drop out within 6 months. This chapter will serve as a road map. As fitness writer David Groves notes in *Self* magazine, "Getting in shape may seem like a solitary battle, but its ups and downs are actually documented and predictable." If you have been on this road before, this chapter will help clarify your experiences. If you haven't, it will point out the obstacles, as well as what you need to run the course successfully.

This road map is based on factors—other than your motives—that come into play when you take on an exercise commitment. Knowing what issues may arise as you make the transition from a sedentary to an active lifestyle will be critical in designing a program that works for you. A fundamental psychological principle tells us:

"behavior = person + environment"

To make changes in your lifestyle ("behavior"), you have to account for who you are ("person") as well as the world you live in ("environment"). Only by considering both parts of the equation will you avoid dropping out and move on toward incorporating fitness in your life.

Dropping out derives in part from not knowing your motives and how you can best achieve them through the right exercise program. That's what we examined in Part II of this book. Another cause of dropping out comes from the unexpected—not knowing what's likely to happen as you enter the novel world of fitness.

A Change in Lifestyle

Developing a commitment to exercise represents a change in lifestyle. As with any change, it can be stressful. This means you may experience doubts and discouragement, or you may feel confused at times. If you start with the belief that exercise is going to make you feel good right away, you could be setting yourself up for failure. Eventually, exercise does make you feel good. Dr. Dorothy Harris says it takes about 12 weeks before fitness improvements are evident, although psychological benefits may be evident as soon as 2 or 3 weeks after starting. Even so, making time for exercise alters the pattern of your life. It can affect relationships with friends and family. According to Dr. Abbey King of the Stanford University School of Medicine, a prime reason for exercise dropout is the threat it poses for the inactive partner.

It takes time to exercise, and before it becomes routine and accepted—by you and others—your life will go through a period of trial and error as you search for the best way to make it work. Until things stabilize, keep your expectations in line and guard against thinking that everything will be wonderful now that you are exercising.

Taking Precautions

There are good reasons for taking every possible precaution to guarantee success in developing the exercise habit. Dropping out leaves a subtle scar of personal defeat—something you believed in, something you wanted for yourself but that you just couldn't stay with. For those who never try, the discomfort is far less. Nothing ventured, nothing lost. But when you put yourself on the line, join a club, sign up for a class, or buy a pair of running shoes, you get real. You acknowledge your needs and take the first step. But then it falls apart. *Why does this happen?*

There are volumes on the topic of exercise adherence analyzing the major factors causing dropout. Poor advisement, unrealistic expectations, and unclear motivations account for large percentages. Of course, there are practical problems like time, money, scheduling, and transportation, but I think that if you are completely honest with yourself, you will acknowledge that where there is a will, there is a way.

So, what makes the difference between the 50% who make it beyond 6 months and the 50% who don't? Where's the magical exercise glue that gets you to stick to your program? To find the answer, we have to examine the path to becoming a regular—and all the potential detours along the way that can produce failure.

The Yellow Brick Road

We can learn a great deal from watching other people—why they succeed and why they fail. And lesson number one is acknowledging that it's easier to learn from other people's mistakes than from our own.

So, what have we learned about the road to successful exercising? How does it develop? What are the steps along the way?

For one thing, we know that habits don't develop overnight and that there are phases or stages we go through in becoming committed to exercise. Going from an inactive lifestyle to an active one is a significant life change that affects us mentally, emotionally, and socially. It is a complex process that takes time and effort to assimilate.

The model I will present was originally developed by Marilyn Taylor of Concordia University in Montreal. It grew out of her efforts to understand how people change. Over my years of working with Dr. Taylor, we have expanded the model to describe the way people take on new life patterns, such as the lifestyle of fitness.

The Four Phases of Change

If at this moment you are feeling content, you are unlikely to change your life just for the fun of it. We call this the *equilibrium* phase. Something has to happen to shake you out of equilibrium and make you feel a need to change. It doesn't have to be something big like getting a promotion or losing a friend. It can be something small that starts things churning. A vague feeling of discomfort may sit beneath the surface until it is stirred by some seemingly trivial comment or event. When this happens, you enter the *disorientation* phase.

Imagine that what shakes you up is something wild like winning the lottery. After the excitement begins to settle down, you need to figure out exactly what winning means to you and what you are going to do with all those millions. This process of thinking things through marks your entry into the *exploration* phase.

It may come suddenly or after trial and error, but sooner or later your search will bear fruit. You will form a vision of what you are going to do and what the change means for you personally. You now enter the fourth phase, *reorientation*, where you begin to implement your plan, making modifications and adjustments as needed. When you feel satisfied with what you are doing, you shift to a *new equilibrium*, coming full cycle but ending up in a different place from which to approach life.

Each of the four phases is characterized by distinct emotional, social, and intellectual experiences. We will review these in the discussion of phases. Also, in moving from one phase to the next, there is something called a *transition* that enables us to make the shift. These transitions are very special and are associated with specific happenings. We will consider the transitions as well. Let's look at the phases again, but this time see how they apply to you in developing the exercise habit.

Transition 1: Moving From Equilibrium to Disorientation

We don't change without reason. Sometimes there is a major eruption in our lives that initiates the change process; other times it is a steady undercurrent that finally breaks the surface in a resolve to action. A visit to the doctor, a progression of dress sizes, or the prodding advice of friends may serve as factors, but in most cases an aspect of our self-image or sometimes our perception of the world gets jolted. Consider the following description of why an acquaintance of mine began to exercise:

> My brother, John, was only 42 when he died—massive heart attack— the result of lots of years of having fun, eating high on the hog, working long hours, and elbow bending with the boys at the local pub. It was then I decided that wasn't going to happen to me. I was 39 at the time. I started running—running for my life—and I haven't stopped since.

People decide to start exercising for a variety of reasons. Some are catapulted from a secure equilibrium by a doctor's firm warning. More often, it just seems that it is the right thing to do and that this happens to be the right time to do it. When our deeper motives are unconsciously concealed from our awareness, the process of developing the exercise habit may be more difficult. That's the advantage you have after completing Part II of this book. Your motives are in the open.

Having analyzed yourself in Part II, you should be more aware of the social, psychological, and body motives that propel your life; this will help you through the four phases of change. It would be a more perilous journey if you were to embark on a new course of action out of a vague feeling of discontent or an incorrect diagnosis of your needs.

Phase I: The Drama of Disorientation

When you put yourself in the fitness world for the first time, you have made it over the first hurdle. You have shifted from a complacent equilibrium to a less comfortable place, but the critical factor is that you made a choice to begin. Now the job is figuring out what to do to stay with it.

Principle 1. Clarify Why You Want to Start!   Sometimes we leap into action too quickly. Review what you have learned about yourself in Part II. What drives you? What dissatisfactions do you have with your life? What would you like to change and why? Look beneath the surface, and take all your motives into account.

Margie was definitely overweight. She made up her mind that she just had to lose 30 pounds. She said she liked clothes and simply couldn't find the dresses she wanted in her size. It wasn't that fitting into a smaller dress size didn't motivate her—there was simply more to it. Like the fact that her husband had become a bit indifferent in the bedroom. Like the uncomfortable feeling about growing old and missing the excitement of her rebellious youth. These things wouldn't alter her goal of losing weight, but being aware of them would help her stick to her plan.

Principle 2. Recognize You Are Shifting Your Identity!   When you are new to fitness, you are likely to experience a kind of identity shift. You find yourself in unfamiliar territory—in a body that may look a bit neglected. Spending time exercising usually places you in a new social network where comparisons could result in feelings of inadequacy. "Everyone else can do things I can't." "Everyone's body looks so much better than mine." Whether or not these observations are true isn't the issue. You may feel out of your league and a bit strange to yourself.

Principle 3. Look to Friends for Support!   Compounding the emotions of an identity shift are reactions from the "old world." People stand a better chance of sticking with an exercise plan if family and friends support their participation. If not, it's all too easy to feel guilty about the time away from home or the other commitments that usually gobble up your hours.

Principle 4. Guard Against Unrealistic Expectations!   Another complication arises from self-expectations about making progress. When you haven't exercised very much in your life, it's easy to believe that once you start, your body will snap right into shape and you will develop a sleek, muscular physique. After all, that's what the ads tell us. "In 3 weeks with just 5 minutes a day. . . . " If that's what drives you to exercise, results will inevitably disappoint you. Changing body proportions takes time and intense commitment, but some novices buy into all the delusions fostered by the media. When reality crashes through to awareness, they start looking for the exits.

Principle 5. Allow Space for Emotional Reactions!   Emotional reactions during the disorientation phase may come in varying degrees and in forms of anger, depression, or despair. You may simmer in self-blame or project anger on others for interfering, for not supporting you, or even for causing you to be in this situation. Anger may give way to a loss of self-confidence and eventually a withdrawal from people related to your discomfort, especially members of your new fitness network. Some people are more private in their emotional reactions, so beware of any tendency on your part to withdraw from others. Even though you may blame yourself or feel hopeless, recognize that these emotions are a normal part of the change process.

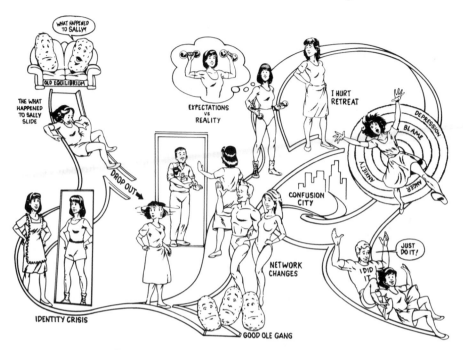

IN THE BEGINNING: THE DRAMA OF DISORIENTATION

Transition 2: Moving From Disorientation to Exploration

The major psychological roadblocks for the novice are feelings of blame and self-reproach. Exercising may confront you with difficult revelations about yourself and your body. All the emotions that get stirred up can make you uncomfortable, and it's much easier to avoid the confrontation than to forge ahead.

To make the transition out of disorientation into the phase of exploration, you have to get beyond blame and self-reproach. You may continue to feel upset, but without feelings of blame and self-reproach you can function more effectively.

How does it work? Giving up self-blame means you no longer need to make excuses for yourself. You start engaging the task—finding out how fitness connects with your life, not someone else's or some idealized version of yourself.

Principle 6. Develop a Constructive Attitude!   If you sum up the beginning weeks of your exercise commitment, there's one word that captures the possible downside of your inner experience—*insecurity*. Your previous lifestyle, friendship networks, and self-definitions may have shifted slightly, leaving you feeling somewhat askew. There is, however, an up side. You have opened up new options for your life, and you get to choose ways of actualizing your life's goals through your personal exercise plan.

It helps to acquaint yourself with others who made it through the phases to develop the exercise habit. All stories are different, but people who made it can show you how to appreciate your discomfort as part of the process and not as something unique to you.

You validate your efforts when you talk to others who have been through this process or who know you and can acknowledge the importance of this new direction in your life. Having someone who can empathize with your uncertainty throughout this identity shift will help you name the problem for what it is—a significant change in lifestyle and values, not just an exercise program that is being scheduled into the week.

All of this may seem extreme. You may be thinking, "Wow! This is a lot to go through. I just wanted to lose a few pounds and tone up my thighs. I didn't realize I was in for all of this!" You have to keep in mind that the goal is lifelong fitness, not just a short-term commitment.

If you look at what it might mean to your life to be exercising *at least every other day of the rest of your life*, you may develop perspective about the magnitude of the change you are contemplating. The goal of losing a few pounds won't be enough to sustain your commitment for the remainder of your life. That's why you went through the process of identifying all your potential exercise motives—so you can build your commitment on a solid foundation. Does it seem more reasonable now that when you are going after lifelong change, your whole identity might be involved?

Phase II: Exploring the Possibilities

Weeks and sometimes months pass before a person brand new to the fitness world begins to realistically address the options and requirements of exercise. If you choose to train at a health club, you will find that most of the advice that is offered may come in the first few sessions and then drop off sharply. This is unfortunate. It's hard for you to keep in mind all the "dos" and "don'ts" of exercise when you are starting. That's why you want to keep your plan simple at the beginning.

Principle 7. Keep Your Plan Simple at the Beginning!   Finding out how you connect with exercise takes time, and it occurs in phases, not all at once. The emotions stirred up during the first phase (disorientation) of developing an exercise habit interfere with making complicated decisions. For this reason, it's best to stick to basics. This means

- start out slowly,
- do things you really like,
- choose activities you are capable of,
- have a clear and simple plan,
- set modest goals you know you can reach,
- anticipate some reluctance to exercise, and
- allow for times when your commitment seems to collapse.

Principle 8. After Establishing the Basics, Open Yourself to the Options!   Once you have worked through the initial problems of starting and are keeping up a regular schedule, you can move onto the agenda of the exploration phase. Now is the time for more sophisticated decision-making about how your motivational profiles relate to fitness options. There is a chance you can lose your commitment at this point if you don't let yourself explore. You can slide out of engagement through boredom and deteriorating interest.

The good news is you are now fit enough to let yourself play in the exercise world—and this is how you will learn about the psychological dynamics of athletics and sports programs. It's an intuitively guided journey to discover what really turns you on, what your deeper needs are all about, and what challenges you want to confront through fitness opportunities.

Michelle had been a competitive skier in college, but gave all that up when medical school consumed her attention. Years later—at the critical age 40 mark—she found herself joining a health club, not out of desire, but out of necessity. An overweight cardiologist didn't set a good example for patients. Most of her time at the club was spent at the juice bar. Exercise simply didn't capture her interest, at least not until she was recruited for a just-for-fun team triathlon. As the cyclist, she surpassed everyone's expectations. More critically, she found herself—or at least that daring, adventurous spirit that she knew from an earlier time. Her workouts changed. They had meaning and purpose. She was *in training* for the summer races.

Principle 9. Join Your Mind With Your Exercising Body!   Ulterior motives have limited staying power. The desire to lose a few pounds or even to live a little longer wears thin on a regimen of boredom and discomfort. You may initiate fitness activities to do something to your body because it has to be done. You may respond to exercise the way a reforming smoker responds to the surgeon general's warnings: Do it or else!

If exercise becomes merely another line on the schedule of life, it won't last. *It has to connect at deeper levels.* If at the end of a workout, you have derived nothing of personal value, the exercise bond weakens, and over time it breaks. I would even go so far as to argue that if in the process of exercising, you aren't emotionally and mentally connected to the experience, the exercise bond dissipates.

The big surprise in the exercise world of the '90s is that body and mind go together as a single package. No matter how you numb it, no matter how high you blast your Walkman or how many magazines you stack on your stationary bike, consciousness remains throughout the workout and determines whether you come back for another round. If you want to develop lifelong exercise habits, you have to take a broader look at the emotional, intellectual, and even spiritual dimensions of exercise and couple these to your exercise program.

This is where your scores on the body, psychological, and social motives play a major role. They may seem abstract when you start your exercise program, but once you are out of the confusion of the disorientation phase and are continuing to exercise, you can begin to explore how these motives connect you to your program.

You must look for the relation between what you are doing in fitness and the values you want to reinforce in your life. You may have identified your motives in Part II of this book, but knowing and experiencing are different. It's when your values are staring you in the face and you are up against the difficult task of trying to honor them that the real work begins. Not only is it more difficult to respect them than you might have imagined, but you may also be confronted with the question of whether this is really what you want. There may be a shifting and sorting of values when you actually try to honor them.

Diane discovered exercise while her marriage was falling apart. At first, it was a bit like dating—it was a diversion from her inner concerns, but it didn't mean much to her. As time passed, she found herself taking long unplanned runs—no goals, no personal challenges, just feeling her changing moods and following her mind's diversions. She spun theories about life, love, and the origins of the universe, while her movements flowed with her thoughts. She came to think of her outings as spiritual journeys, never as workouts. She said they satisfied her soul.

Transition 3: Moving From Exploration to Reorientation

The flashbulb theory of insight suggests a sudden awareness. The rheostat theory represents a more gradual awakening. As you explore your inner

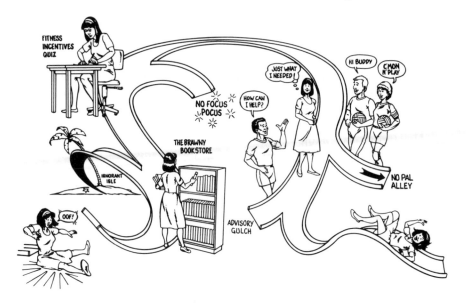

FIGURING IT OUT: THE WORK OF EXPLORATION

relationship to your exercising body, you will come to appreciate what excites you—and the potential exercise holds for helping you achieve personal goals. This may come suddenly, but more typically it is a growing awareness.

Principle 10. Insight Empowers You to Be Your Own Exercise Coach! It's another kind of adolescence as you come to understand yourself in the exercise world. You feel less dependent on others for support and advice. You may even withdraw from some of your newfound exercise buddies as a way of "flying solo." This is a point where you begin to experience things jelling.

Harry couldn't exercise without his trainer. Even though he ran his own business, he simply couldn't recall what he did from one workout to the next. He just followed his trainer's directions every time. When his trainer was unavailable, he still went to the club, but he hung around like a lost child. The whole thing puzzled him, but it took months of talking to insightful friends and reading books on health and psychology until he began to understand his curious relationship to exercise and his body.

The conclusion Harry came to was that he was out of touch with his body. He treated it like his car, taking it in for medical checkups and keeping it tuned by going to the gym. For the most part, he lived in his head, which, incidentally, had served him well by making possible a comfortable lifestyle. But something was missing. He started exercising as a reflection of a deeper, but unconscious, discontent with his life. His gradual awakening was fostered by paying attention to his curious exercise behavior. When he came to understand how much he had denied his body over his lifetime, he realized that he needed to become more integrated—mind and body—in order to *feel fully alive*. Harry developed his own exercise program and eventually gave up his trainer. It was a natural and healthy progression.

Phase III: Reorienting Your Life in the Exercise World

A complaint about traditional psychoanalysis is that it mainly develops insight—and at best, insight gets you only halfway there. The work of the reorientation phase is that of implementing the program and getting the bugs out. It means trying it out for real and making adjustments when necessary.

At this stage, your needs become more concrete. Sometimes it's a need to find a class schedule that meshes with other demands. It might be something as specific as making a better babysitting arrangement. At this point, you have the determination to work things out, to accommodate fitness as part of your life. But things can still go wrong.

By the time you reach the reorientation phase, you may have anywhere from 2 to 6 months of training behind you. People vary greatly in how long it takes to meet the challenges presented by each phase. As you put the finishing touches on your exercise commitments, you have surpassed the early hurdles of aching muscles and joints but must now face possibilities of overuse and more chronic problems. Staying with a dance exercise class five times a week requires up-to-date information about things like class content, proper posture, and aerobic footwear. Exercising the habit over a long period of time requires intelligence so you can continue to enjoy yourself and remain injury-free. This is where advisement reenters the scene.

Principle 11. Technical Information Is Essential to Progress!   As the exercise habit takes hold, feedback about the technical aspects of your workouts becomes essential. In your struggle to become regular, you may not have been as concerned with the "right way" to exercise. Take running as an example. It seems like a natural enough activity, but there are ways of doing it that are anatomically better for you. Seasoned runners are acutely aware of the equipment they use, namely, their shoes. Most can deliver sophisticated lectures on the problems of pronation or supination—but can they accurately analyze their own body dynamics in running? It's unlikely, unless they have asked for feedback from an expert.

Experts can help you analyze your performance, correct your movements, and show you how to avoid injury. This point came through loud and clear one day when I was working out on the treadmill at my health club. A trainer came by and commented on my pattern of running. I had defined myself as an endurance athlete years ago, and most of my running workouts had the quality of being long—and slow.

The following day, the trainer arranged to run with me, but according to his plan. We started with a slow warm-up of 15 minutes at a pace of 8 minutes per mile. That was about as fast as I usually ran, though I typically kept it up for an hour or more. After a 2-minute break, we then ran a 6:30 mile. Halfway through, the trainer asked me how I was doing. I said I was dying. He commented with a smile, "You look plenty alive to me." That meant I had to finish. And I did. Five minutes later, we started in again—interval training. Two minutes on at a 5:30 pace, 2 minutes rest. After two of these, I wanted to go home. We did five. To finish off, we ran three intervals of 1 minute at a 5-minute pace and 1 minute of rest.

We continued this routine over the next few weeks, and what amazed me most was that I could run that fast. I simply didn't know that about myself. When I asked the trainer why he wanted to change my program, he said he thought I was in a rut. My technique was fine, but I was holding myself back and not reaching my potential. Since that was one of my needs, I greatly appreciated his intervention. I could not have changed without his help.

Transition 4: Moving to a New Equilibrium

There are times throughout this personal change from being inactive to becoming active when you need people, or more accurately, you need specific kinds of input from specific people. There are also times when you need to reflect privately. As you enter the ranks of the "regulars," you may feel a desire to mark this graduation by sharing your excitement and your experiences. You may find a renewed interest in talking about yourself in relation to exercise. You just want to tell people about your changes, to share with them your journey, and perhaps to make yourself available in helping others who are on their way to developing the exercise habit.

Phase IV: Establishing a New Equilibrium

The journey ends as you enter a new equilibrium, one that is characterized by a commitment to your exercising self and a stability in your patterns of fitness involvement. As always in periods of equilibrium, we try to preserve the harmony and balance earned through our efforts, at least until it no longer suits us. And then the rumblings are felt, the stirrings deepen, and—who knows—perhaps the birth of a master athlete is in the offing.

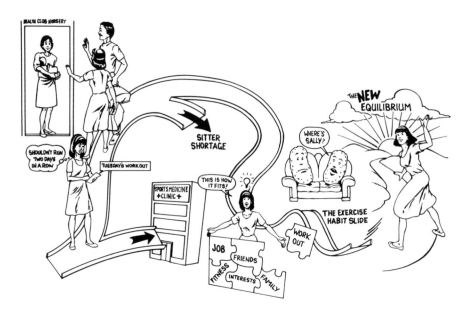

MAKING IT WORK: THE EXCITEMENT OF REORIENTATION

Coming Full Circle

As changes take hold at deep levels in your life, it feels as if they have always been there. This makes it hard to appreciate all the confusion and emotional turmoil you went through to make it happen. There are people who wake up one morning and decide to exercise for the rest of their lives, and that's what they do. When they tell their stories, they usually leave out all the internal dialogue they had with themselves for years beforehand to make this sudden change come about. All they describe is the moment of change. It makes it sound so simple, or it makes the person seem so remarkable. In either case, we are misled.

There is a pattern by which we accommodate changes in our lives. It's like navigating the globe, in that we travel far away from our point of origin only to return to ourselves with new experiences and a new self-understanding. Our journey into the fitness world may seem so desirable at the outset. Yet, as we embark on our adventure, we are confronted with unanticipated emotions and circumstances. The journey grows perilous. In persisting, we achieve a deeper understanding of who we are, and eventually what seemed so foreign becomes an old and valued friend.

There is a paradoxical sensation of newness and familiarity when we make significant changes in our lives. The sense of familiarity comes from knowing that we have only fulfilled our deeper selves in accomplishing these changes, bringing ourselves more to the surface. That's why the fitness incentives are so important to developing the exercise habit. We recognize ourselves in them and, through our commitment to exercise, witness our self-actualization.

CHAPTER 8

KNOWING AND HONORING YOUR COMMITMENT

"Where the heart is willing, it will find a thousand ways, but where it is unwilling, it will find a thousand excuses."

DAYAK PROVERB

Awareness and Responsibility

"Ignorance is bliss." One of the risks of self-awareness is that you can't play dumb any more. If you know what you need, you have to deal with the question of what you are doing about it. You can't say, "Oh, that's not important to me!" Knowing your needs and realizing how you can satisfy them through a fitness commitment will empower you to move ahead in life—to make a quantum leap from ineffectual ways of addressing your life's agenda to ways that really work. Of course, you can continue to debate whether you have the right to your needs or whether you are capable of making good things happen for yourself. Sooner or later, however, you have to face yourself and acknowledge that there is no valid reason not to try—and the only option is to start exactly where you are.

What Are Your Excuses?

Sure, there are always excuses. But why would you make excuses? Why would you neglect your needs? Let me guess some of the answers:

1. It's too hard.
2. It takes too much time.

3. I can't afford it.
4. I'd feel self-conscious.
5. I lack support from family and friends.
6. I'm too tired.
7. It's too late to start to exercise.

Excuse #1: It's too Hard

Here's a typical expert's reaction to a beginner's complaints about the difficulty of exercise: "If it's too hard, you are approaching exercise the wrong way. You have to go slowly at first and gradually build up strength and endurance." That makes sense, but it leaves something out—like the fact that sometimes it hurts to exercise.

People who have been exercising for many years can get a little pious, sort of like reformed smokers. Tell the truth. How often do you see people smiling as they bench press 200 pounds or as they run a subminute 440? That kind of exercise hurts. But I'm concerned with a different kind of hurt, because you can always lower the weights or slow your pace. It's the kind of hurt I sometimes feel when I begin tying on my running shoes. I have spent whole mornings walking around the house with one running shoe on and the other in my hand, arguing with myself about whether I really want to go out and have a "fun run." Some days it's difficult to start. I listen to the dialogue in my head. It sounds like my mother telling me I'm going to love brussels sprouts. Miraculously, though, it changes—once I start. It's no longer brussels sprouts, it's pizza and ice cream without the indigestion. And it gets easier the more "starts" you have behind you. You know the transformation is for real—you can count on it.

If it helps, feel free to grit your teeth. Grumble and complain. Moan out loud. And then—go for it. Change is hard. Commitment is hard. Reaching distant goals is hard. It feels like a struggle. Some people overcome inertia with a little power of positive thinking; others like to make sounds resembling an old engine starting up. Whatever you need to get you going, use it—because *hard* is not a dirty word.

I think we sport experts do novices a disservice when we tell them it's going to be easy. It's true that few experts still believe in the "no pain, no gain" theory or the idea that exercise has to hurt. You can get fit without incurring physical pain. But you may still experience psychological pain—the anguish of change, the effort to sustain determination, and perhaps underlying it all, the liking yourself enough to continue doing something that is totally for yourself.

Excuse #2: It Takes too Much Time

Experts offer two well-worn arguments against this objection. The statistical one is that people who are extremely busy with family, work, and social obligations still find time to exercise. Moreover, once they have developed the exercise habit, they wouldn't dream of dropping it. Exercise helps them keep their lives in balance. Illustrating this point, Dr. James Rippe, a cardiologist and the director of the American Health Fitness Institute, surveyed 1,139 chief executives and found that 64% of them exercise regularly. That's six times the participation rate for American adults.

"I'VE GOT TOO MUCH TO DO. I DON'T HAVE TIME TO EXERCISE."

The second argument is a practical one that tells us that exercise doesn't have to mean going to the health club for 2 hours a day. It can be 15 minutes of t'ai chi in the morning and another 15 minutes before bedtime. Or it can be walking to work instead of taking the bus.

Both of these arguments are valid, but there's another important point to consider. If you had a choice of enjoying lunch with good friends at an open-air cafe or pounding out 5 miles on a treadmill, what would you choose? Be honest. Sure, you can readjust your schedule, manage your time better, and knock off those time-consuming Saturday afternoon naps, but *why*? That's the real question.

If push comes to shove, so to speak, you can always find the time. But to find it, you have to want to and know *why* you want to. Having analyzed your motives, you are now equipped with all the answers you need to the question why. Some of your payoffs will be long-term, not like the immediate pleasures of lunch or a nap. So, a bonus benefit of exercising is that it develops your ability to delay immediate gratification and go after the long-term benefits of a healthy lifestyle.

The bottom line is that the time is there, hidden away in poor scheduling or implicit choices about things you would rather do. It's deciding to change your priorities that makes time appear.

Excuse #3: I Can't Afford It

True. The last pair of running shoes I bought cost over 100 bucks. I can't afford that. My car tires are cheaper, and they come with 20,000-mile guarantees. What running shoe will give you that much guaranteed smooth riding? What makes it worse is that I have to buy a different pair of shoes for walking, for cycling, for aerobics classes, and for basketball, not to mention the special shoes I need for windsurfing. And this is only the beginning. Once upon a time, I wore an all-purpose sweatshirt, jock strap, and shorts. Now I have to get outfitted for running in a spandex ensemble, buy a special aerobics suit, have a wetsuit for swimming and windsurfing, and heaven help me if I don't wear padded cycling shorts.

"YOU KNOW, YOU'VE GOT TO HAVE A LOT OF MONEY THESE DAYS TO GET INTO EXERCISE."

Tell me I don't need these things. Did Greg LeMond wear cutoff shorts in the Tour de France? Did Dave Scott wear his old "tennies" in the Ironman? Did Florence Griffith-Joyner run the 100 in an old sweatshirt?

I haven't even registered at the health club, and already I'm broke. This fitness stuff is big business, and I can't afford it. Just when I think I have caught up with the fitness fashion, it changes.

Well, the positive side is that since I have so much money invested in this gear, I might as well use it. So I do.

I should be the last one to give advice on this point. I get hooked by all the gadgets and high-tech ways of shaving seconds off my cycling times. It has been an insidious transformation. I started making deals with myself. Pinching my pennies on eating out in exchange for those new "double bubble" running shoes. One year, I even gave up renting videos for a windsurfer. Now, I'm working on a single sculling boat (I won't tell you what I'm giving up for that).

But I have to be honest. I really don't need all these things. It's just my way of having fun. Being a fitness regular for over a quarter-century means that I have accumulated a little paraphernalia. I didn't have these things in the beginning, and I know I would continue to exercise without them now. They just make up part of my ritual. They help me identify with my goal.

When you look at it closely, fitness is pretty inexpensive entertainment. Maybe a little music for an at-home workout. Good footwear for a walk or a run. A lot of people make their own weights by filling plastic jugs. The most critical item is one you can't buy—it's the motivation to do it. So now that you have that, what are you waiting for?

Excuse #4: I'd Feel Self-Conscious

Perhaps you would feel embarrassed because you think your body is too fat, too thin, not muscular enough, or just not *right*. I can identify with that. I went to Gold's Gym one time and felt like the 99-pound skinny weakling in the old Charles Atlas ads. I'm closer to 180, so you can imagine what these guys and gals looked like. When I was going through another phase in my long and winding exercise history, I had to confront more basic matters. It was in a modern dance class that I learned I couldn't distinguish my right foot from my left. And then there was the problem of hiding my love handles in a leotard. Can't be done, not when you're wearing a "dance belt" (a jock in other contexts) that works like a tight rubber band around a marshmallow.

Some people deal with it by getting up at 5 a.m. and exercising in the dark. That's not my style. My body likes slow, easy movements in the morning. So, maybe long sweatshirts would work—the kind that go all the way down to my knees.

Perhaps I'm skewing this a little. When I get distracted from my goals, I pay more attention to what I look like than what I feel like. My mind mixes up what's important, substituting an external focus for an internal one. On days like this, it may take a little extra effort to push away my self-consciousness. Predictably, the more I get into my workout, the less self-conscious I feel.

A sense of humor helps when you are having a "crisis of confidence." Be prepared. Get yourself a T-shirt with the slogan "You Should Have Seen Me in My Former Life" painted on it. Exercise with a friend who has an "I could care less!" attitude. Acknowledge that "this too shall pass"—and just get on with it.

The fact is that the vast majority of people who exercise are probably your biggest fans. They have no vested interest in putting you off. After all, you are joining them in something they believe in. You are just a new kid on the team, and although there may be some initiation rites, if you continue to "show up for practice," you will get the respect you deserve. People will acknowledge you for trying, and in time your body will look and feel better to you.

Excuse #5: I Lack Support From Family and Friends

This can be a real problem. When you start changing yourself for the better through exercise, family and friends can get pretty jealous. It's similar to the loving husband who heaps mashed potatoes on his wife's plate while she's dieting. Her getting thin threatens him. Your getting fit may threaten somebody close to you.

I have a friend whose wife encouraged him to join a health club to deal with his stress. But then she got extremely jealous because he started taking aerobics classes with seminaked women. Before things came to a head, my friend surprised his wife with a club membership so she could take aerobics with him.

People we love can be our greatest allies or our worst enemies when we are beginning to exercise. After all, if the modern health club is the yuppie substitute for the bar scene, there's some risk that all those spandex outfits will get you panting for the wrong reason. If your friends and family are a little self-conscious about their bodies, it's no wonder they might feel threatened by your sudden interest in fitness.

Here's a great statistic. Psychiatrist Victor Altshul from Yale University Medical School hypothesized that if a lean, athletic man is consciously or unconsciously contemplating divorce, there will be at least a 75% chance that he is, or will be, a compulsive runner. This isn't the kind of fitness data your lover wants to hear.

It's a double-edged sword. On the one hand, you can question why people who are supposed to love you would object to your doing something good for yourself. On the other hand, you have to be sensitive to their needs, recognizing they may feel abandoned by you, that you have switched sides and now belong to the opposition. Knowing how difficult it has been for you to get started and become regular may help you be more sympathetic to their fears. Besides, if you can invite them to join you, it might make it better all around.

Excuse #6: I'm too Tired to Exercise

This also is true for me. I am not a morning exerciser. My body refuses to move fast before noon, regardless of how much caffeine I give it. By the time I have finished my day, I feel drained. Even though it's emotional fatigue, my body feels dead. What a dilemma! I guess it's the law of inertia: "Bodies at rest tend to stay at rest." My body doesn't want to move, never mind exercise! My mind colludes and tells me I'm tired.

Fortunately, I learned a lesson a long time ago. On days when I feel fatigued, I may need exercise the most. It's a simple relationship. 2 + 2 = 4. A tired mind plus a good workout equals reincarnation. The truth is I'm not physically tired. I have been sitting most of the day or making small trips around home or office. It's also true that it takes time to shake off mental fatigue. If I go to the health club, I may amble from one machine to the next in halfhearted gestures until my body begins to revive. I feel like a sputtering engine that has to be kick-started over and over. Once I get moving, it's ecstasy. Occasionally my engine won't turn over. When that happens, I do something more in tune with its needs. A slow swim. Some yoga. A half hour of t'ai chi. There is always some movement that's right for my needs. Knowing the importance of reacquainting my mind with my body each day has led me to develop lots of alternatives for when my mind gets stubborn and absolutely refuses to take my body running or when aerobics classes look like a Woody Woodpecker film on fast forward.

There's also the opposite problem of your body being tired from honest physical labor. Then you may need something different from exercise in its customary interpretation. Your body may need to stretch out or be taken for a refreshing walk. Even here, we have to be careful about the mind playing tricks on us. When I was in my 30s, I was involved in some psychological studies of underground miners. I figured that the best way to understand this lifestyle was to live it. So that's what I did for a couple of summers. It was hard work, especially because I was at the bottom of the labor ladder. I was tired when I finished my shift, but oddly enough I still had enough energy for a run each day. In a way, my body demanded it. It felt good to work my breathing up to a steady rate and blow off the fatigue. I usually felt more energized after my runs than before them.

To put it bluntly, I think most of the fatigue we feel in modern life is more mental than physical. It's a psychological hurdle we have to jump. The more we experience the boost we get from exercise, the more we can request that our minds take a break while we stealthily tie on our workout shoes or slip into the locker room.

Excuse #7: It's too Late to Start to Exercise

If this is a subtle form of ageism, I would rather answer the objection by referring anyone who feels this way to a local meeting of the Grey Panthers. Stand up and tell them, "Old people shouldn't exercise." By the way, make sure you stand close to the exit when you start speaking.

Maybe it's not that you feel too old, but rather that you feel too something else—too out of shape, too fat, too emaciated, and so on. I think by now you know my answer. Yes, it's hard. People may stare. You might feel uncomfortable. But, it's worth it—and it gets better all the time.

"I'M JUST TOO OLD TO START EXERCISING."

Choosing Health

I acknowledge that my responses to typical excuses for exercise avoidance are superficial. It's difficult to overcome the arguments our minds present to maintain the status quo. Change is by definition unsettling. I have spent so little time on objections to exercising because I believe the real task is finding your reasons *to* exercise.

When I was first starting out in psychology, I waded through a quagmire of definitions of mental health in search of something that made sense to me. I read definitions that filled entire books and ones that concluded that mental health can't be defined.

My search ended in 1969, while I was attending a seminar conducted by Harvard psychologist Dr. Chris Argyris. He offered an intriguing definition of mental health. First, he said a mentally healthy person operates out of rational self-interest. Second, he indicated that if a mentally healthy person were presented with valid information showing how her behavior was inconsistent with her rational self-interest, she would correct her behavior.

It took me a while to figure out what Dr. Argyris was saying, but when I did, it seemed straightforward. His definition offered a concrete way of knowing whether some action of mine was mentally healthy or not. Take, for example, the behavior of smoking. Start with valid information: Cigarette smoking has been strongly related to lung cancer. Now for rational self-interest: I don't want to get lung cancer. Put them together. If I want to minimize my chances of getting lung cancer, I don't smoke. This doesn't mean that all smokers are mentally unhealthy, but they have one strike against them, especially if they say they don't want to get lung cancer. I think the same reasoning applies to things like unsafe sex, driving without a seatbelt, consuming high-cholesterol foods, and even the assiduous avoidance of exercise.

In making the fitness connection, a major complication is not being clear with yourself about your needs or, in Dr. Argyris's terms, your rational self-interest. In the light of day, you have examined your needs in earlier chapters and hopefully have seen how these needs can be met in the exercise world. You may not care about being slim or even about living to a ripe old age. But what is it that you do care about? What have you identified that is important for you to pursue?

Experts tell us that mental health is not simply the absence of mental illness—it is the presence of high-quality functioning, sometimes referred to as self-actualization. One way it has been portrayed is on a continuum from health to illness with normalcy in the middle.

HEALTHY ———————————— NORMAL ———————————— SICK

It's interesting to look at things this way. It explains how, for instance, people live in limbo, functioning according to the "norms" for our times or our culture, but not making an effort to become fully healthy or need-fulfilling. So, it's "okay" to get fatter as we grow older (on the average, 1 pound per year) because that's the norm—or to have a couple of drinks per day, because many people do it and some doctors say it's okay.

It's a real risk to put yourself on the line and go after what you want. It takes courage, commitment, and a clear sense of purpose.

Waiting—for What?

Addiction columnist John Bradshaw, writing in *Lear's* magazine, explored the magic of waiting in people's lives—"the idea that if you just wait long enough, something good will happen." He discussed the case of an 85-year-old woman who was extremely angry because, having been divorced at age 43, she had waited 42 years for the rest of her life to begin—and nothing had happened. Bradshaw speaks to the point: "We need to live in reality and to understand that there is absolutely no magic in waiting. All good things do *not* come to those who wait. . . . We need to sit down and decide what we want in life and begin to envision those goals and the way we intend to go after them. The only time to wait is when we have no alternative. Waiting has no intrinsic causality. And it can ruin lives." A friend of mine complained about the spawning fat cells in her thighs. This was over 10 years ago, and at the time I suggested she begin an exercise program. She reasoned that it was too late to begin and magically wished they would just go away. I argued that it was only going to get worse—and so it did. Now, she grabs the folds of flesh on her legs and says, "What am I going to do?" I respond, "My answer is the same. What are you waiting for?" Her eyes roll toward the heavens, and she sighs whimsically, "I don't know. Something, I guess."

Sometimes we delude ourselves into thinking we need things a certain way before we can act. We witness it when students sharpen their pencils, tidy their desks, arrange their files, and conjure up all kinds of "necessary" tasks so that studying always becomes the "next" thing on the list. Or we listen to people who plan a divorce—when the kids are grown, when they have their own income, or when they have resolved all their emotional agendas. Procrastination gets raised to a high art form. We make promises to call an old friend, to have a medical checkup, to quit smoking, to take a vacation. And tomorrow is always a better day to start.

We wait for the right time, the right circumstances, the right whatever it is that we think will make it happen easily, painlessly, and without the slightest disruption to our carefully balanced lives. The magic of waiting lures us with false belief that wishing is having and thinking is doing. And we succumb because at heart we doubt ourselves or fail to understand that self-love doesn't always take the path of least resistance.

Your Exercise Mantra

Here's one last challenge. Can you put together what you have learned in a simple message—a statement of purpose?

"I'm doing this to stay healthy."

"I need to sharpen my competitive edge."

"Exercising will make me more self-confident."

Unfortunately, these sentences might not sound right to you. You need a very personal statement, so unless it's yours, it won't have the ring of truth. What you need is a personal *mantra*: a saying you can repeat to yourself to get you out the door and over the hurdles of internal and external resistance—a saying that is an affirmation of who you are now and who you are in the process of becoming.

This isn't the same as goal setting. It's a statement of your commitment to yourself. You can't always rely on "being in the right mood" or "feeling like it" to get you into the locker room. I often talk to people who drop their fitness programs for periods of time because they forget what it's all about or because they start checking whether they feel like exercising. Count on it, there will be plenty of days you won't want to exercise—and doing it when you don't want to isn't about being masochistic. It's about commitment to yourself.

I mentioned earlier that few exercise specialists believe exercise has to hurt in the physical sense. Yet if it were so easy, most people would do it. So we know where the hard part is. It's in the practice, or the discipline. There's an old saying that good things in life don't come easily—you have to work for them. For the most part, this is true. One of the latest gimmicks in the fitness market are machines that do it for you. All you do is strap yourself in and turn the machine on. The rest is done for you. But what is being done for you? Precious little. By definition, exercise is work you do. You can't hire a personal trainer to do it for you or buy exercise videos and hope that watching will be enough.

There's another saying I like. It comes from the biography of Joe Clark, an inner-city high school principal, depicted in the film "Lean on Me." It's a classic:

"Discipline is not the enemy of enthusiasm!"

Let's come back to the idea of an exercise mantra. *Mantra* is a Sanskrit term referring to a mystical formula of incantation. It's a phrase you repeat to yourself to bring forth something you desire. In the practice of meditation, a person repeats a word or phrase over and over to transcend the normal state of mind and enter into an experience of inner stillness. The mantra helps quiet the mind's chatter by forcing it to focus on this one expression. The meditator becomes single-minded—in harmony with the mantra. All distractions or conflicting agendas are shut out by focusing on the mantra.

It isn't like arguing with yourself. If you listen to your chattering mind, especially when you are thinking about exercising, you will hear a heated debate about the whys and why nots. Adding one more why will just increase the chatter by provoking a counterargument.

A mantra isn't something you debate, but something you accept as valid for yourself. Through repetition the mind is focused on a single intention. The chatter may continue. The mind may want to argue. But if you are clear about your intention, there is nothing to debate. The mantra is a simple statement of purpose.

A good example of an exercise mantra comes from a friend of mine who was well motivated to exercise but nonetheless had difficulty getting out of bed at 5:30 three mornings a week. Understandably so. Jennie told me she was a hedonist and loved being on the receiving end of praise, particularly about her looks. Her vanity motivated her to exercise, as did her interest in health, youthfulness, and stress management. She knew how extremely important exercise was to her and acknowledged that it would always be part of her life. Even so, 5:30 came too soon some mornings.

Having her workout bag ready helped, but what got her out the door was the promise she made. For years, Jennie drifted through life like a ship without a rudder. She was swayed by momentary needs and, as a consequence, couldn't count on herself to follow through on important commitments. She knew all the reasons why exercise was good for her, but couldn't find the glue. That was before she realized how committing herself to exercise would allow her to practice taking charge of her life. Being reliable to her exercise program became a critical element in the rebuilding of her self-esteem and self-trust. It was a training ground where she could demonstrate over and over her self-control. Her exercise mantra was the statement, "I need this to show I'm in control and reliable to myself." It came in the form of a thought as she looked at her bag by the door and heard her mind tempt her with an extra hour of sleep. In the 2 years following her realization of this commitment, she hadn't missed a single workout.

I can't offer you a list of sentences from which to choose. This is a very private piece of work. I am convinced, however, that if you have been conscientious in assessing yourself throughout the earlier sections of this book, you will have learned some important things about yourself. You may be struggling right now, trying to make sense of all these discoveries—and that is how it must be. Reflecting on all you have learned and then distilling the ingredients to come up with your essential truth is the task you must address now.

You may wonder how you can boil it all down into one sentence. Let me help. You have evaluated yourself on 18 separate motives and seen how each can support your involvement in exercise. You have connected your primary motives to specific programs of exercise, and understood why these activities are best suited to your needs. I am not asking you to lose track of any of this, but rather to dig deeper. Just as Jennie knew why she wanted exercise in her life, you have that knowledge as well. What she needed, and what I believe we all need, is an orienting purpose. Call it a bottom line or a guiding star, it is a self-realization about what really counts and what you are truly committed to.

Ordinarily, I don't spend much time debating with myself about whether I want to work out. I have pretty well scheduled my days so that I know when I am going to exercise and have a reasonable idea about what I am going to do. But when the exercise hour arrives, I can hear the internal debate. It may be faint, it may be a whine, sometimes it's a roar, but it's usually there. I may remind myself that this a decision I already made. But deep inside there is another message that is partly verbal and partly feeling. The voice inside lets me know that this is important, that I work out so I can be the best of me, so I can be true to all my goals. The feeling is equally convincing, like hands embracing inside, confirming my commitment. As I leave my office, my body turns right toward the club instead of left toward home. It may seem automatic, but it isn't. It took a lot of self-understanding to get here, and then making the commitment to stand behind the things I want for myself.

Making It Happen

The final tying together of all the pieces should be an affirmation of your intentions and your plan. In chapter 6 you identified your primary motives, and you matched exercise programs to them. In chapter 7 you mentally ran the obstacle course leading to exercise compliance. In this chapter you have worked toward identifying a deeper orienting purpose for exercising. What you need to do now is write down all you have learned.

The summary form provided in Table 8.1 is a way of putting together in one place the major things you have learned. Answer the questions as a way of making your commitment explicit. When you're finished, cut it out and put it somewhere you will see it often. You can tuck it into your date book, hang it on the refrigerator, glue it to the mirror in the bathroom, or memorize it and repeat it to yourself daily. Know that it's yours—and that you mean every word of it.

Table 8.1 Making It Happen

---

1. What are my motives for exercising?

---

a) As a way of recapturing your motivations, list in the spaces below your top three HIGH MOTIVES that you identified in chapter 6. Simply write the names of the three motives.

HIGH MOTIVE #1 _____
HIGH MOTIVE #2 _____
HIGH MOTIVE #3 _____

b) To help you keep track of other motivational considerations, you were asked in chapter 6 to identify three LOW MOTIVES that concerned you. What were those three motives? Write the names in the spaces below.

LOW MOTIVE #1 _____
LOW MOTIVE #2 _____
LOW MOTIVE #3 _____

(Cont.)

Table 8.1 (Continued)

---

2. What exercise program or sport activities best suit my motives?

After reviewing your motives in chapter 6, you were guided through a series of questions (see Figures 6.2-6.7 for motive analyses) to help you pinpoint the best exercise program for your needs. You were asked to write down your FIRST CHOICE for activity and ALTERNATIVES that also appealed to you. Look at the activities you listed as First choice and alternatives in chapter 6 and write them down in the appropriate spaces below:

Your First Choice:

Alternatives:

3. What actions do I have to take *now*?

Consider what you need to do now. You may need to schedule an appointment with your doctor. You may need to talk with your spouse or other family members. Perhaps you need to call up some of the fitness clubs in your area for information.

On the checklist below, check items that you need to do now and write down a specific date by which you want to complete this agenda.

Example: To do	**By when**
____ **Call local fitness centers**	**November 1**

To do	**By when**
____ Have a physical exam	
____ Review my finances	
____ Talk to spouse/partner	
____ Discuss fitness plans with family	
____ Discuss fitness plans at work	
____ Discuss fitness plans with friends	
____ Check out local fitness centers	
____ Research equipment/shoes	
____ Set up a tentative exercise schedule	
____ Buy equipment/shoes	
____ Find an exercise partner	
____ Locate a personal trainer or coach	
____ Other _____	

4. What's my orienting purpose—my mantra?

To make your mantra clear, write down your deepest sense of what exercise means to your life, what you want from it, and why you are doing it. Make your statement as clear and simple as you can.

"YOU'VE COME A LONG WAY, BABY!"

SOURCES

Abraham, H., & Joseph, A. [Cited in Porterfield, K.M. (1989, October). Endorphins: The brain's natural opiates. *Cosmopolitan*, pp. 50-51.]

Abraham, S., & Johnson, C.L. (1980). Prevalence of severe obesity in adults in the United States. *American Journal of Clinical Nutrition, 33*, 364-370.

Ainsleigh, G. [Cited in Green, L. (1989, May). Endurance tests. *Self*, pp. 162-166.]

Altshul, V.A. (1981). Should we advise our depressed patients to run? In M.H. Sacks & M.L. Sachs (Eds.), *The psychology of running*. Champaign, IL: Human Kinetics.

American Academy of Physical Education. (1989). *Physical activity and aging*. Paper No. 22. Champaign, IL: Human Kinetics.

American College of Sports Medicine. (1983). Proper and improper weight loss programs. *Medicine and Science in Sports and Exercise, 15*, ix-xiii.

American College of Sports Medicine. (1986). *Guidelines for graded exercise testing and exercise prescription* (3rd ed.). Philadelphia: Lea & Febiger.

American College of Sports Medicine. (1990). *The recommended quantity and quality of exercise for developing and maintaining cardiovascular and muscular fitness in healthy adults*. Indianapolis: Author.

American College of Sports Medicine. (Undated). *Position stand: Weight loss programs*. Indianapolis: Author.

American Heart Association. (1990). *1990 heart and stroke facts*. Dallas: Author.

Anderson, O. (1989, January). A run a day keeps the doctor away? *Runner's World*, pp. 54-57.

Bennett, W., & Gurin, J. (1982). *The dieter's dilemma: Eating less and weighing more*. New York: Basic Books.

Berk, L. [Cited in Pierpont, M. (1989, March). Future fitness? Mind health. *Self*, pp. 141-146.]

Blair, S.N., Kohill, H.W., Paffenbarger, R.S., Clark, D.G., Cooper, K.H., & Gibbons, L.W. (1989). Physical fitness and all-cause mortality. *Journal of the American Medical Association, 262*, 2395-2401.

Blumenthal, J. [Cited in Cimons, M. (1988, July). Futile attraction. *Runner's World*, pp. 38-46.]

Bouchard, C., Shephard, R.J., Stephens, T., Sutton, J.R., & McPherson, B. (Eds.) (1988). *Exercise, fitness, and health: The consensus statement.* First International Conference on Exercise, Fitness, and Health, Toronto, May 29-June 3.

Bradshaw, J. (1990, July). The futility of magical thinking. *Lear's*, p. 50.

Brant, J. (1987, May). And the word was aerobics. *Runner's World*, pp. 68-76.

Cash, T.F., Winstead, B.A., & Janda, L.H. (1986, April). The great American shape-up. *Psychology Today*, pp. 30-37.

Centers for Disease Control. (1989). Progress toward achieving the 1990 national objectives for physical fitness and exercise. *Morbidity and Mortality Weekly Report*, **38**, 449-453.

Chan, C. [Cited in Grant, E. (1988, May). The exercise fix. *Psychology Today*, pp. 24-28.]

Chernin, K. (1985). *The hungry self: Women, eating, and identity.* New York: Times Books.

Chinnici, M. (1990, April). Eat less and live longer? *Self*, pp. 174, 211-212.

Cisar, C.J., & Kravitz, L. (1991, January). Turning back time: Exercise and aging. *Idea Today*, pp. 28-35.

Cleary, P.D., Miller, M., Bush, B.T., Warburg, M.M., DelBanco, T.L., & Aronson, M.D. (1988). Prevalence and recognition of alcohol abuse in a primary care population. *American Journal of Medicine*, **85**, 466-471.

Coplan, N. [Cited in Brown, K.C. (1990, June). Moderation is best. *Shape*, pp. 100-101.]

Cousins, N. (1979). *Anatomy of an illness as perceived by the patient: Reflections on healing and regeneration.* New York: Norton.

DeBusk, R.F., Stenestrand, U., Sheehan, M., & Haskell, W.L. (1990). Training effects of long vs. short bouts of exercise in healthy subjects. *American Journal of Cardiology*, **65**, 1010-1013.

Desai, Yogi Amrit. (1983, Summer). Fitness: Tool for inner transformation. *Kripalu Yoga Quest.*

DeVillers, L. [Cited in Bluestone, M. (1990, June). The exercise stimulant. *Longevity*, p. 92.]

de Vries, H. [Cited in Livermore, B. (1989). Is it chemistry or body heat? *Health*, pp. 50-56.]

Dienstbier, R. [Cited in Kaufman, E. (1989, November). The anti-stress power of exercise. *Self*, pp. 166-168.]

Dishman, R.K. (1987). *Exercise adherence: Its impact on public health.* Champaign, IL: Human Kinetics.

Dishman, R.K., Sallis, J.F., & Orenstein, D.R. (1985). The determinants of physical activity and exercise. *Public Health Reports*, **100**, 158-171.

Drawbridge, J. (1990, June). Swimming's longevity payoffs. *Longevity*, pp. 44-46.

Drewnowski, A., & Yee, D. (1987). Men and body image: Are males satisfied with their bodies? *Psychosomatic Medicine*, **49**(6), 626-634.

Dychtwald, K., & Flower, J. (1989). *Age wave*. Los Angeles: Tarcher.

Elis, S. (1989, June). Anti-aging news. *Longevity*, pp. 11-14.

Elman, J.B. (1986, July). The loneliest of the long-distance runners. *Runner's World*, pp. 34-39.

Experts focus on sex addicts. (1990, May 22). *Montreal Gazette*, p. C1.

Eysenck, H. (1988, December). Health's character. *Psychology Today*, pp. 28-35.

Feineman, N. [Cited in Pierpont, M. (1989, March). Future fitness? Mind health. *Self*, pp. 141-146.]

Flannery, R.B. (1990). *Becoming stress resistant: Improved well-being through the Project SMART system*. New York: Continuum.

Flippin, R. (1987, March). Are runners better lovers? *The Runner*, pp. 32-36.

Francis, P., & Francis, L. (1988). *"If it hurts, don't do it."* Rochlin, CA: Prima.

Frankl, V.E. (1971). *Man's search for meaning*. New York: Washington Press.

Frauman, D. [Cited in Leonard, G. (1989, May). Sex and other pleasures: The case for pleasure. *Esquire*, pp. 153-156.]

Friedman, M., & Rosenham, R.H. (1976). *Type A behavior and your heart*. New York: Knopf.

Glasser, W. (1976). *Positive addiction*. New York: Harper & Row.

Glassner, B. (1988). *Bodies: Why we look the way we do (and how we feel about it)*. New York: Putnam.

Griest, J.H., Klein, J.H., Klein, M.H., Eischens, R.R., Gurman, A.S., & Faris, J. (1979). Running as a treatment for depression. *Comparative Psychiatry*, **21**, 611-619.

Groves, D. (1989, February). No-quit fitness. *Self*, pp. 74-76.

Gwinup, G. [Cited in Stockton, W. (1988, March 30). Study suggests exercise is key factor in successful dieting. *Montreal Gazette*.]

Hales, D., & Hales, R.E. (1985). *The U.S. Army total fitness program*. New York: Crown.

Hales, R. [Cited in Flippin, R. (1987, March). Are runners better lovers? *The Runner*, pp. 32-36.]

Harris, D. [Cited in Sims, S.M. (1990, January). The future of fitness is now. *Self*, pp. 105-111, 148-150.]

Haskell, W.L. (1984). Overview: Health benefits of exercise. In J.D. Matarazzo, S.M. Weiss, N.E. Miller, & S.M. Weiss (Eds.) *Behavioral health: A handbook of health enhancement and disease prevention*, pp. 409-423. New York: Wiley.

Helmreich, R. [Cited in Katz, S.J., & Liu, A.E. (1990, January). The success trap. *Self*, pp. 100-104.]

Hirschman, J.R., & Munter, C.H. (1989, November). Feeling fat: Is it an emotional issue? *New Woman*, pp. 148-152.

House, J. [Cited in Hall, H., Roberts, M., King, P., Greene, C., Adessa, M., & Cassell, J. (1988, November). People who need people. *Psychology Today*, p. 8.]

Howes, L. [Cited in Pierpont, M. (1989, March). Future fitness? Mind health. *Self*, pp. 141-146.]

Hunt, M. (1974). *Sexual behavior in the 1970s*, Chap. 3. Chicago: Playboy Press.

Kaplan, J. (1989, September). Slaves to the scale. *Self*, pp. 192-195.

Kaufman, E. (1989, December). Put some muscle into it. *Shape*, pp. 123-129.

Khantzian, E. [Cited in Gelman, D., Drew, L., Hager, M., Miller, M., Gonzales, D.L., & Gordon, J. (1989, February 20). Roots of addiction. *Newsweek*, pp. 52-57.]

Kiev, A. [Cited in Flippin, R. (1987, March). Are runners better lovers? *The Runner*, pp. 32-36.]

King, A. [Cited in Solomon, S. (1989, April). When exercise doesn't promote love. *Psychology Today*, p. 14.]

Koplan, J.P., Caspersen, C.J., & Powell, K.E. (1989). Physical activity, physical fitness, and health: Time to act. *Journal of the American Medical Association*, **262**, 2437.

Kostrubala, T. (1976). *The Joy of Running*. Philadelphia: Lippincott.

Kostrubala, T. [Cited in Flippin, R. (1987, March). Are runners better lovers? *The Runner*, pp. 32-36.]

Landers, S. (1990, March). Phobias: A stepchild garners new respect. *APA Monitor*, p. 18.

Lane, N.E., Wood, P.D., Bloch, D.A., Jones, H.H., Marshall, W.H., Jr., & Fries, J.F. (1986). Long distance running, bone density, and osteoarthritis. *Journal of the American Medical Association*, **255**, 1147-1151.

LeBow, F. [Cited in Gambaccini, P. (1989, February). Love on the run. *Runner's World*, pp. 34-37.]

Leonard, G. (1989, May). Sex and other pleasures: The case for pleasure. *Esquire*, pp. 153-156.

Leonard, G.B. (1974). *The ultimate athlete: Re-visioning sports, physical education, and the body*. New York: Viking Press.

Lobstein, D. [Cited in Cardozo, C. (1990, February). Getting your anger out. *Self*, pp. 151-155.]

Lynch, J. [Cited in Green, L. (1989, May). Endurance tests. *Self*, pp. 162-166.]

McArdle, W.D., Katch, F.I., & Katch, V.L. (1986). *Exercise physiology: Energy, nutrition, and human performance*, (2nd ed.). Philadelphia: Lea & Febiger.

McClelland, D. [Cited in Justice, B. (1989, November). The ties that heal. *Better Homes and Gardens*, pp. 48-51.]

Minden, H. [Cited in "Making friends motivates people to keep fit." (1983, October 22). *Montreal Gazette*, p. C3.]

Mole, P.A., Stern, P.A., Schultz, C.L., Bernauere, E.M., & Holcomb, B.J. (1989). Exercise reverses depressed metabolic rate produced by severe caloric restriction. *Medicine and Science in Sports and Exercise*, **21**, 29-33.

Morgan, W. [Cited in Johnsgard, K.W. (1990, April). Peace of mind. *Psychology Today*, pp. 73-81.]

Morgan, W.P., & Goldston, S.E. (Eds.) (1987). *Exercise and mental health.* Washington, DC: Hemisphere.

Nagler, W. [Cited in Sims, S.M. (1990, April). Dr. Nagler says "Keep moving." *Self*, pp. 165-169.]

National Sporting Goods Association. (1989). *NSGA Predicts 5% Growth for Sporting Goods in 1989.* Mt. Prospect, IL: Author.

National Sporting Goods Association. (1989). *1989 Sports Participation.* Mt. Prospect, IL: Author.

National Sporting Goods Association. (1989). *Lack of time and self-discipline primary excuses for out-of-shape Americans.* Mt. Prospect, IL: Author.

North, G. (1989, July). Exercise. *Cosmopolitan*, pp. 92-93.

Nosenchuk, T.A. [Cited in Padgett, V.R., Chong, W.K., & Trulosn, M.E. (1985, January). That mild mannered Bruce Lee. *Psychology Today*, p. 79.]

O'Shea, M. [Cited in Kaplan, J. (1988, July). Fitness crazy. *Vogue*, pp. 222-226.]

Paffenbarger, R.S., Hyde, R.T., Wing, A.L., & Hsieh, C. (1986). Physical activity and all-cause mortality, and longevity of college alumni. *New England Journal of Medicine*, **314**, 605-613.

Prussin, R. [Cited in North, G. (1989, July). Exercise. *Cosmopolitan*, pp. 92-93.]

Rippe, J.M. (1989, May). Fitness: The performance plus. *Psychology Today*, pp. 50-53.

Schmais, C. [Cited in Starzinger, P.H. (1989, May). Balance of power. *Self*, pp. 96-100.]

Seid, R. (1989). *Never too thin: Why women are at war with their bodies.* New York: Prentice Hall.

Seid, R. [Cited in Tucker, S. (1990, July). What is the ideal body? *Shape*, pp. 95-101, 112-114.]

Self-esteem Self survey. (1990, June). *Self*, pp. 26-28.

Seligman, M.E. (1980). *Human helplessness: Theory and applications.* New York: Academic Press.

Seligman, M.E. (1988, October). Bloomer blues. *Psychology Today*, pp. 50-55.

Selye, H. (1975). *The stress of life* (2nd ed.). New York: McGraw-Hill.

Shames, L. (1989, May-June). Running on empty. *New Age Journal*, pp. 58-60.

Shames, L. (1989). *The hunger for more: Searching for values in an age of greed.* New York: Time Books.

Sharpe, R. [Cited in Drawbridge, J. (1990, June). Swimming's longevity payoffs. *Longevity*, pp. 44-46.]

Shephard, R.J. (1990). *Fitness in special populations*. Champaign, IL: Human Kinetics.

Siegel, M., Brisman, J., & Weinshel, M. (1988). *Surviving an eating disorder*. New York: Harper & Row.

Sims, S.M. (1990, January). The future of fitness is now. *Self*, pp. 105-111, 148-150.

Solomon, H.A. (1984). *The exercise myth*. New York: Harcourt Brace Jovanovich.

Sonstroem, R.J., & Morgan, W.P. (1989). Exercise and self-esteem: Rationale and model. *Medicine and Science in Sports and Exercise*, **21**, 329-337.

Stamford, B.A., & Shimer, P. (1990). *Fitness without exercise*. New York: Warner Books.

Steinbaum, E. (1989, April). Fear of fitness: The real reasons some women don't work out. *Self*, pp. 113-116.

Stephens, T., & Craig, C.L. (1990). *The well-being of Canadians: Highlights of the 1988 Campbell's survey*. Ottawa, Canada: Canadian Fitness and Lifestyle Research Institute.

Sutton, R. (1987). *Body worry*. New York: Viking.

Tavris, C. (1982). *Anger: The misunderstood emotion*. New York: Simon & Schuster.

Tavris, C. [Cited in Cardozo, C. (1990, February). Getting your anger out. *Self*, pp. 151-155.]

Tucker, S. (1990, July). What is the ideal body? *Shape*, pp. 95-101, 112-114.

U.S. Public Health Service. (1990). *Healthy People 2000*. Washington, DC.

Vejnoska, J. (1989, September 15). U.S. children becoming less fit. *USA Today*, p. 1A.

Wallace, R.M. (1990, May). Twenty-five years of women's fitness. *Cosmopolitan*, pp. 185-202.

Weinshel, M. [Cited in North, G. (1989, July). Exercise. *Cosmopolitan*, pp. 92-93.]

Whitten, P., & Whiteside, E.J. (1989, April). Can exercise make you sexier? *Psychology Today*, pp. 42-44.

Williams, R. (1989). *The trusting heart: Great news about Type A behavior*. New York: Time Books.

Williams, R. (1989, May-June). The trusting heart. *New Age Journal*, pp. 26-30.

Wise, E. (1990, July). Feeling fat. *Shape*, pp. 20-21.

INDEX

ABOUT THE AUTHOR

James Gavin, PhD, has been a practicing psychologist since 1969 and is the author of *Body Moves: The Psychology of Exercise*. He is also a professor of applied social science at Concordia University in Montreal and an adjunct professor of psychology at Colorado State University.

Gavin is a member of the American Psychological Association's exercise and sports psychology division and of the American Board of Professional Psychology. He is a featured speaker at many national and international conferences. He is also a committed athlete himself, enjoying competitive swimming, modern dance, triathlons, windsurfing, and instructing aerobics and yoga.